CHURCH AND STATE
IN EDUCATION

By

WILLIAM CLAYTON BOWER

THE UNIVERSITY OF CHICAGO PRESS
CHICAGO · ILLINOIS

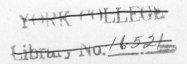

THE UNIVERSITY OF CHICAGO PRESS · CHICAGO
Agent: THE CAMBRIDGE UNIVERSITY PRESS · LONDON

PREFACE

THE contents of this volume were originally given as the James R. Richard Lectures in Christian Religion at the University of Virginia in November, 1943. In suggesting that the lectures for 1943 should be devoted to a discussion of religion in education, the Committee on Public Occasions has selected one of the most pressing problems in contemporary American life from the point of view both of religion and of the life of the nation. The problem is old as far as American culture is concerned. In the recent past, however, it has assumed new aspects and a new and insistent urgency. There are indications that it may become, if it is not already, one of the central problems in American education.

Needless to say, the problem is extremely complex, and the solution is fraught with many difficulties. But, whatever the difficulties may be, the problem of religion in education needs to be faced forthrightly as a matter of public policy in the interests both of the children and young people of the nation and of the nation itself. The problem has not been created by the present national crisis, but it is greatly accentuated by it.

The problem needs to be studied afresh in the light of a century and a half of American experience and in the light of cultural change in a highly dynamic society. Particularly there needs to be a re-examination of the fundamental concepts underlying the problem—the relation of church and state, the nature and ends of education as a social process, and the functional relation of religion to personal and social experience.

Certainly there could be no more appropriate setting in

[iii]

which this problem could be discussed than in the university founded by Thomas Jefferson and under the shadow of Monticello.

The lectures as they were originally given have been somewhat expanded and rearranged for purposes of publication.

If in the present discussional stages of the subject what is set forth in the following pages will help to formulate the problem, to place it in its cultural context, to clarify it, and to suggest possible directions in which its solution may be sought, the purpose of this volume will have been fufilled. In a problem so manifestly difficult of solution there will need to be a meeting of many minds holding different points of view, both religious and social, and beyond the stages of formulation and hypothesis much patient and wisely guided experimentation in many different types of community.

My thanks are due to Mr. Thomas Franklin Freeman, Fellow in the Divinity School of the University of Chicago, for arranging the Bibliography, as they are to Associate Professor Nelson B. Henry, of the Department of Education of the University of Chicago, for suggesting valuable sources. I acknowledge with thanks the permission of the Abingdon-Cokesbury Press to develop a point of view initially formulated in chapter iv of *Christ and Christian Education*.

W. C. B.

Lexington, Kentucky
November 1943

TABLE OF CONTENTS

I

AN OLD PROBLEM IN A NEW SETTING

1–21

II

THE EDUCATIONAL SITUATION IN AMERICA

22–40

III

FUNDAMENTAL ASSUMPTIONS

41–56

IV

TOWARD A CONSTRUCTIVE SOLUTION: THE SCHOOL

57–77

V

TOWARD A CONSTRUCTIVE SOLUTION: THE CHURCH

78–95

A SELECTED BIBLIOGRAPHY

96–99

INDEX

101–3

I

AN OLD PROBLEM IN A NEW SETTING

IN THE light of a growing expression of concern on the part of public school authorities, churchmen, and public officials, it is quite clear that one of the crucial problems confronting the educational leaders of America is the relation of religion to education in a democracy. As a matter of course, throughout the nation's history this has been a concern of churchmen, though for them the specific nature of the problem has assumed different forms in different periods of American life. In the recent past, however, this concern has found expression in the philosophy and psychology of education.[1] In widely different parts of the nation, including some of the largest metropolitan centers, churches have made overtures to public school authorities and public school authorities have made overtures to churches to offer religious instruction in relation to the programs of the public schools on time released from the public school schedule, with or without credit. This arrangement has recently been carried to the high-school level. Of late, instances have occurred in certain localities where courses in religion are offered by teachers specially trained in the field of religion and certified by the state, in public school property, as an integral part of the school's curriculum but with salaries paid by the churches. In a number

[1] Cf., e.g., J. C. Chapman and G. S. Counts, *Principles of Education* (New York: Houghton Mifflin Co., 1924); Robert Ulrich, *Fundamentals of Democratic Education* (New York: American Book Co., 1940); Daniel A. Prescott, *Emotion and the Educative Process* (Washington, D.C.: American Council on Education, 1938); and G. W. Hartman, *Educational Psychology* (New York: American Book Co., 1941), esp. chap. xii, where emphasis is placed upon values.

of instances instruction in religion has been completely incorporated in the school's program on the same basis as general science, history, literature, and the arts under state support and supervision.

The concern of public school officials regarding the place of religion in education is unequivocally enunciated in the Tenth Yearbook of the Department of Superintendence of the National Education Association:

> Our society today awaits a new integration of knowledge, aspiration, and human purpose which will take into account the findings of science, the theory of evolution, the fact of material abundance, and the growing power of the laboring classes, as well as the influence of great spiritual leaders. Until such an integration is forthcoming, the present condition of moral chaos is likely to continue and the more fundamental problems of character education will defy solution. Whether this is the task of the church or some other agency we cannot say today; but it would seem to be a task that is essentially religious in nature.[2]

In giving its commission to the White House Conference on Children in a Democracy in 1939, the President of the United States, enumerating the needs of children with which the Conference was directed to deal, said:

> We are concerned about the children who are outside the reach of religious influences, and are denied help in attaining faith in an ordered universe and in the fatherhood of God. . . . . I look to you for comprehensive review of the problems before us, and for suggestions as to practical ways in which we may advance toward our goal.[3]

For the first time in the history of the White House conferences that of 1939–41 included religion. Failure to include it in earlier conferences was due, no doubt, in part to the highly controversial nature of the problem and in part to a difference in orientation toward the nature and urgency of the problem. In this conference the consideration of religion was

---

[2] *Character Education* (Washington, D.C.: Department of Superintendence, 1932), p. 23; cf. also pp. 35–36, 190.

[3] *Conference on Children in a Democracy: Papers and Discussions at the Initial Session* (Washington, D.C.: U.S. Department of Labor, 1939), pp. 4 and 5.

given a place on an equal basis with housing the family, economic resources of families and communities, economic aid to families, health and medical care of children, education through the school, social services for children, children in minority groups, child development through play and recreation, libraries, and child labor and youth employment. No part of the report received more meticulous and concerned attention than that on religion and children in a democracy. The Conference expressed its profound conviction as to the importance and urgency of dealing with the problem constructively:

Practical steps should be taken to make available to children and youth through education the resources of religion as an important factor in the democratic way of life and in the development of personal and social integrity. To this end the Conference recommends that a critical and comprehensive study be made of the various experiences both of the churches and of the schools in dealing with the problem of religion in relation to public education. The purpose of such a study would be to discover how these phases of education may best be provided for in the total program of education, without in any way violating the principle of the separation of church and state.[4]

These are unmistakable evidences of a new awareness of the problem created by the exclusion of religion from public education when it is one of the most fundamental functions of democracy. They are evidences of a new attitude toward the problem. Perhaps they are evidences that, as the outgrowth of the cultural change that has been so characteristic of American culture through more than a century and a half of national history, our generation is confronted by a problem that in many of its essential aspects is new. In any event, whether the present concern grows out of a new sensitivity to an old problem or out of the pressure of a problem that is in many respects new, we face an anomalous situation that grows more

[4] *Proceedings of the White House Conference on Children in a Democracy* (Washington, D.C.: U.S. Department of Labor, 1940), p. 31.

and more intolerable and about which something must be done.

It is not without significance that the problem in its present form does not arise merely or chiefly out of the interests of ecclesiastical groups, which in the past have tended to think of themselves as the custodians and exponents of religion; though undoubtedly, to a certain extent at least, certain of these groups would be glad to see their interests furthered by some alliance with the public school. On the contrary, it arises out of a concern of the community for the needs of children and young people, on the one hand, and for the needs of the nation, on the other. By this rootage of the problem the issue is shifted from its older center of ecclesiastical sectarianism, or even church and state relationships, to the area of community welfare and of public policy.

This reorientation toward the problem of the relation of religion to education arises out of the fact that in its present form the problem presents itself as the outgrowth of a century and a half of national history. The conditions and character of American life have undergone great changes during that period, brief as it is as national histories go. American life began with the founding of the thirteen colonies along a narrow strip of territory on the Atlantic seaboard in the seventeenth century. The settlers who founded these colonies brought with them their European backgrounds of thought, institutions, and social customs. These included not only their religious and political but their social and educational ideals as well. For a considerable time the colonies were separate and independent social and political units. Only gradually and in response to emerging common needs did they achieve a loose confederation. Not until nearly a half-century after they had broken with the mother-country and had adopted a formal constitution did they develop what might be considered a national consciousness.

The severance of ties with Great Britain involved much more than the Revolutionary War. It was a psychological process involving considerable time and the operation of many factors, social and intellectual as well as political. An understanding of the European backgrounds of thought and life which for so long dominated the Colonial scene and in reaction to which many of the basic ideals and structures of American life developed is necessary to an understanding of the formulation of the ideas and attitudes that furnished the foundational structures of early American culture. These ideas and attitudes did not spring into existence full-grown. They had a natural history and were the outgrowth of concrete historical processes involving adjustments to specific situations. Once this insight is achieved, it is clear that provisions that were made in the early phases of the growth of the American nation were relevant to the then existing conditions and must be re-examined from time to time in the light of new situations that have developed in the course of the changing American scene.

In no respect is this truer than in regard to the fundamental concepts that are involved in the consideration of the problem of the relation of religion to education—the concepts of the nature and ends of education in a democracy, of the nature and function of religion, of the relation of church and state, and even the concept of democracy itself. The content, spirit, and organization of education, which for a considerable time followed the inherited pattern of European education, were gradually modified under the growing demands of an expanding national culture within the conditions of the unique American situation. Religion, even though establishment was for a time perpetuated under the Congregationalists in New England and under the Anglicans in the southern colonies, was to develop, under the conditions of the frontier and migrant groups, a sectarian pattern of independent ecclesiastical groups of relatively equal status, each strenuously contending for its exclusive interpretation of theology as supernaturally revealed in the Holy Scriptures. (The concept of the separation of church and state and the guaranties of religious freedom were worked out in reaction from church establishment and church interference with the state through the long centuries of struggle between these two institutions in Europe. This basic reaction was greatly accentuated in America by the disruption of the schools through the teaching of opposing sects and the attempts of the sects to control the schools.) Even the concept of democracy itself was the outgrowth, not only of a reaction against the tyranny of British rule, but of the opposing conceptions of the rule of the people and the rule of a landed aristocracy and a growing industrial plutocracy, as expounded by Jefferson and Hamilton.

One who has not followed closely its development in recent years may scarcely be aware of what has happened in the religious situation in America, particularly since the beginning of the present century. As long as religion was thought of in terms of sectarian theology and ecclesiasticism, the problem of the relation of religion to education in a democracy was insoluble in any terms other than the exclusion of religion from general education. But, as the result of cultural change, views regarding the nature and function of religion as well as its structural organization have undergone profound modification. The social conditions that gave rise to sectarianism have changed, so that the grounds upon which it rested have to an increasing extent become anachronistic and unrealistic. As a result, the sharp lines that once separated the sects have for some time been in the process of decay. The general public and the denominations themselves have less and less interest in theological differences that had their origin in issues no longer relevant to contemporary life, and the denominations are coming to stress their common convictions and responsibility to society. This is evidenced by the large-scale movements toward the organic union of formerly exclusive sects, such as the Congregationalists and the Christians, the Cumberland Presbyterians and the Presbyterians, the Free Baptists and the Northern Baptists, the various branches of Lutheranism, and the United Church of Canada. Conversations have for some time been under way looking to the uniting of bodies holding more widely divergent views regarding theology and polity, such as the Congregationalists and the Presbyterians, and the Presbyterians and the Episcopalians. It is further evidenced by the various forms of interdenominational co-operation in local community and national enterprises, such as city church federations, state councils of churches, the home and foreign missions councils, and the Federal Council of the Churches of Christ in America, representing twenty-three of the major Protestant communions. Its most recent expression is the emergent ecumenical idea, which had its beginning in the Lausanne Conference on Faith and Order and the Stockholm Universal Conference on Christian Life and Work, was greatly furthered by the Oxford and Edinburgh conferences, and has eventuated in the organization of the World Council of Churches.

These are unmistakable signs of the movement of Protestantism toward corporateness. As the late Dean Shailer Mathews observed:

It is apparent that denominations sprang from experienced need and are the outcomes of economic and political conditions which have largely disappeared. The various religious bodies conserve a common religious faith and, with the exception of a few of the smaller bodies, all but identical theologies. . . . . The theological struggles which played so large a role in the sixteenth and seventeenth centuries are becoming anachronistic. Denominations are feeling the integrating process of the modern world. . . . . Outside of small sects, differentiation within Protestantism is being replaced by co-operation, and denominationalism, like democracy, is passing from the individualistic to the social stage. There is, in fact, often wider difference

[7]

between members of the same denomination than between denominations themselves.[5]

Even Protestants, Catholics, and Jews have found common grounds of co-operation in such movements as the Church Peace Union, the World Alliance for International Friendship, the National Council of Christians and Jews, and the White House Conference on Children in a Democracy. In the White House Conference report a joint statement on religion and recommendations that a commission be created to study the relation of religion to education in American democracy were prepared by an interfaith section. In Chicago, in response to a proposal of the superintendent of schools to release time and extend credit for religious instruction by the churches and synagogues at the high-school level, an interfaith committee was created and worked together in complete harmony.

From the standpoint of education the most significant of these co-operative movements is the International Council of Religious Education. Through this council, representing forty-one denominations and more than 85 per cent of the Protestant communicants of the United States and Canada, the denominations have, since 1922, been co-operatively engaged in the formulation of aims, curriculum, methods, and standards, with a professional advisory section on the co-operation of community agencies, including the public school. In this council official representatives of the co-operating denominations work together on the common tasks of religious education and interpret religion, not in sectarian terms, but in terms of a common faith that transcends all denominational differences. In its official statement of its basic philosophy and policy religious education is interpreted in terms of the fundamental values involved in divine-human relations and is in no

[5] W. C. Bower (ed.), *The Church at Work in the Modern World* (Chicago: University of Chicago Press, 1935), chap. iii, "The Co-operation of the Churches."

[8]

sense construed as indoctrination in some sect or creed but rather as the creative development of attitudes and values.[6]

At the same time that religion in America has been moving away from its traditional theological and sectarian stereotypes, it has become more and more sensitive to personal and social values. Once concerned almost exclusively with sectarian theologies and practices, it has become concerned with the wider ranges of intellectual, economic, political, aesthetic, and ethical values, as evidenced, for example, by the "Social Creed of the Churches" formulated by the Federal Council of the Churches of Christ in America and by the voluminous social pronouncements of the several communions, together with the recent emergence of social reconstruction as a fundamental objective of religious education. At the same time, as religion has moved toward the conservation and creation of values, it has come to be recognized by an ever widening constituency within the churches that much which was formerly classified as "secular" has profound religious significance, as in the case of social ethics. Thus, to the modern religious thinker the sharp distinction between the "religious" and the "secular" has tended to disappear in what is felt to be a continuity of operative values in every dimension of human relations.

In the meantime, while the forces of history have been cutting the ground from beneath sectarianism, more than half a century of the scientific study of religion, as is pointed out in chapter iii, has resulted in a functional concept of religion. The outgrowth of researches in anthropology and ethnology and in the history, philosophy, and psychology of religion has been an unmistakable trend in the direction of seeing religion as a phase of culture operating within the area of man's valuational experience. Since the beginning of the century the

[6] *Christian Education Today* (Chicago: International Council of Religious Education, 1940).

trend has been to identify religion specifically as the revaluation of all values—intellectual, economic, social, political, aesthetic, and moral—into a total meaning and worth of life.[7] A differentiation is thus made between the universal function of religion as an integrating process in personal and social experience and the intellectual concepts (theology), institutional structures (ecclesiasticism), and practices through which the function has been instrumented by various sects. This is the concept of religion adopted in the present discussion and upon which its proposals are based.[8]

As is to be expected in this, as in all social phenomena, sectarianism still continues as an anachronistic expression of religious life in America. To many members of the churches religion still continues to be identified with Presbyterianism, Lutheranism, Congregationalism, Methodism, Catholicism, and Judaism, along with numerous other sects. But any realistic historical approach clearly recognizes such identification of the function of religion with sectarian theology and polity as a survival which lags far behind the operation of the social forces of American culture and the growing insights of informed religious thinking. To ignore these changes in the understanding of the nature and function of religion would be comparable with ignoring the changing concepts of atomic structure, the principle of relativity, the development of economic concepts since Ricardo, or the significant changes in educational theory and practice just because they are not as yet generally understood or accepted by the popular mind. Education rests its theory or practice not upon popular sur-

[7] W. C. Bower, "Religious Education and the Psychology of Religion," *Religious Education*, January, 1928, pp. 7–19; also "The Nature and Function of Religion," *ibid.*, April, 1936, pp. 95–99 (report of the findings of a group of historians, philosophers, and psychologists professionally engaged in the study of religion).

[8] For the elaboration of this conception of religion as a basic assumption upon which the solution of the problem is based, cf. chap. iii.

vivals or prejudices but upon the results of research, insight, and experimentation. Nothing less is demanded in dealing with religion as an integral phase of personal and social experience.

The basic concepts of the "American dream" were dynamic, not static, concepts. Their roots were deep in the soil of the concrete historical situation of the seventeenth and eighteenth centuries. They arose in part out of the social tensions between the newborn nation and its European backgrounds and in part out of the social tensions within the emerging nation itself, as between the industrial North and the agrarian South and between the conservative seaboard population and the advancing liberal frontier. They are, therefore, to be thought of as operational values and ideals of the initial period in an evolving national process. They must be understood and judged in the light of their social and historical context, and not as given and rigid forms which are merely to be perpetuated in their formal details under the changed and changing conditions of contemporary American life. Their meaning and value were not exhausted, or even fully apprehended, by the historical period that gave them birth. Rather, they are living and dynamic ideals that need to be re-examined, reformulated, extended, and deepened in the light of the growing experience of the American way of life on the field of an expanding national history.

Since the period of its beginnings, the nation has expanded from the thirteen original colonies along the Atlantic seaboard to include the vast domain of an almost empty continent— across the fertile plains of the Mississippi Valley, the wide-extending prairies of the West, the Rocky Mountain region, and the Pacific Coast lands; from the Gulf of Mexico to the Canadian border and beyond to include Alaska, Hawaii, Puerto Rico, the Philippines, Guam, Samoa, the Panama Canal Zone, and the Virgin Islands. The population, exclusive of the colonial possessions, has grown from slightly more than one and a half million at the time of the Revolution to more than one hundred and thirty millions. The center of population has steadily moved westward from some point near the Atlantic Coast to Sullivan County, Indiana.

With the occupation of the continent and the growth of population the biological and ethnic character of the American people has greatly changed. During the early phases of colonial and national life the American people were homogeneous as to both language and race. The earliest settlers came chiefly from Great Britain, with comparatively small groups from Scandinavia, Germany, Holland, and France. The earliest immigrants continued to come in an increasing stream from the English-speaking peoples and from northern European stocks of kindred race. But with the rapid growth of industry not only was the volume of immigration greatly augmented but by the middle of the nineteenth century its sources had shifted to central, eastern, and southern Europe. These new sources of population brought to the growing nation widely different racial, cultural, political, and religious heritages. Thus the American people have in the course of a century and a half become the most heterogeneous in the history of mankind. Through the processes of interracial and intercultural assimilation there has emerged an extremely vigorous and versatile people.

As a result of the technology growing out of the application of the methods and results of science to practical operations, American society has undergone a radical process of industrialization. Not only has this changed the basic national economy, but it has also profoundly affected the American way of life. America began its career as a predominantly agricultural society. It was the early conviction of Thomas Jefferson that the success of the American experiment in democracy depended upon an agricultural economy in which free men

[12]

would till their own land. To his dismay, however, during his own lifetime he was to see the process of industrialization well under way, with growing tension between the manufacturing North and the agrarian South and West, accompanied by profound political changes. Subsequent to his death this transformation was to proceed until America has become a predominantly industrial nation.

The repercussion of industrialization upon the structure of American society has been profound. Industry, concentrated around power-driven machinery, gave rise to the city, with a corresponding concentration of population. By 1920 more than half the American people lived in cities. Here the great majority of immigrants from central, eastern, and southern Europe, with their widely variant heritages of race and culture, were congregated. Meanwhile, rural life was impoverished by the movement of its people from farms to factories and from self-sufficiency and independence rooted in the soil to landless dependence upon wages. There was thus created what in Europe had come to be known as a proletarian class, while wealth and power were concentrated in the hands of the few. Between these upper and lower economic classes the great middle class has tended to disappear, with tenantry in the country developing simultaneously with a proletariat in the city. The mechanized and impersonal life of the city has created an entirely different orientation toward the values and processes that constitute the common life. Of late the influence of urban concentration upon the birth rate has begun to appear. The mechanized city is not biologically reproducing itself. The national population is being maintained by a differential birth rate in the rural sections, particularly in the South and in the intermountain region.

Simultaneous with the progress of industrialization and its profound effects upon the character and structure of American society, another change of far-reaching consequences for the American way of life was taking place. It was the disappearance of the frontier. Undoubtedly the frontier, more than any other single factor, was influential in shaping the early American mind. The unexplored possibilities that always hovered over unoccupied land bred a quality of optimism and adventure. Firsthand contact with nature and struggle with its elemental forces created a spirit of initiative, resourcefulness, and independence notably characteristic of the American temper. This contact and this struggle furnished the fertile soil for the indigenous American philosophy of pragmatism and experimentalism. The frontier is also largely responsible for the practical attitudes of rugged individualism and laissez faire. But the frontier passed with the occupation of the last remnants of productive land. At the remotest boundaries of the national domain the American people were turned back upon themselves and were confronted with the necessity of conserving and making the most of such natural resources as they already possessed. The disappearance of the frontier called for attitudes and habits new to the American people. The American dream of a boundless future was beginning to shape itself to the realities of a limited sphere of operation.

In the meantime, what was once a collection of separate and independent colonies, states, and regions is rapidly becoming a national *community*. This is due in part to the closure of the frontier. It is due in part to the technological development of the means of production, communication, and transportation. It is due in part to the fact that production and distribution have become national in their scope. The sources of raw materials and markets have ceased to be local or even regional. Large-scale processing operations draw raw materials of many kinds from many and distant sources, and their finished products are consumed under modern systems of merchandising in every part of the nation. Laws regulating interstate com-

merce have been necessary to govern the flow of goods across state boundaries to distant points of consumer needs. Gradually there has emerged a national economy calling for social planning that includes a balanced production of both farm and manufactured goods in relation to national needs. Public health, nutrition, housing, and education have become national concerns and will remain so as long as a third of the American people are "ill-housed, ill-clothed, and ill-fed." The conditions of the sharecropper and the dweller in the city slums have become the responsibility of the whole American public. New social problems, undreamed of by the Founding Fathers and national in their scope, have arisen within the evolving life of the nation. The nation has become a vast *community* of common interests and closely interrelated functions. To meet the demands of these new social realities the American people of our generation have now to achieve new corporate attitudes and techniques of living together co-operatively as the Founding Fathers had in their generation to achieve liberty and the basic structures of the new republic.
(Under the influence of these social changes the concept of democracy itself is undergoing extension and enrichment. The American way of life is a unique experiment in democracy. Democracy, however, is not a static concept. It is a process, a becoming, in which new possibilities of relations and functions are constantly emerging as the experiment unfolds under changing conditions. It was inevitable that in the beginning emphasis should be placed upon the freedom of the individual and that the primary function of government should be to guarantee his "inalienable" right to "life, liberty, and the pursuit of happiness." Consequently, that government was thought to be best which governed least. It now becomes clear, however, that corporateness, co-operation, and responsibility are as essential to a stable and effective democracy as is personal liberty.) The constructive contribution of the new

collectivistic and totalitarian systems in other contemporary societies lies in the fact that they have achieved corporate unity, though at the cost of individual freedom. The constructive contribution of democracy lies in its emphasis upon liberty, often at the cost of unity. Neither liberty nor unity is a valid concept when dissociated from the other. In their isolation they are both self-destroying. Their validity consists in their interrelatedness as complementary and mutually supporting phases of a corporate society of free persons. In the meantime, democracy, which in the beginning was construed primarily in political terms, is gradually being extended to industry, education, the equalization of opportunity, and the rights of minority groups.

At the very moment when the nation is becoming a close-knit, interdependent community, it finds itself thrust into the midst of international relationships of unprecedented magnitude and complexity. In the earlier and simpler days of the frontier the nation was a self-sufficient social unit, secure in the possession of its vast resources and defended by the natural barriers of two broad oceans. It is no longer so. At the same time that independent states and widely divergent sections were being fused into a national community, the nations, cultures, and races of the world were being lifted out of their isolation and brought into ever closer and more interdependent relationships. A planetary society was in the making, with all the accompanying tensions and adjustments which such a process involves. World War I was a tragic symbol of this accomplished fact. It was a symptom, not a cause, though it greatly accentuated the process. To the surprise of all and the dismay of many, the nation discovered how deeply and inevitably it had become a participant in a world society, with all the responsibility which such participation involves. Until Pearl Harbor the theory of isolationism lived on as an anachronistic survival of attitudes that had grown up out of the frontier period but that were no longer realistic. It is the judgment of not a few observers that our refusal to accept this relationship and its attendant responsibilities in helping to create an international structure that would insure a just and durable peace was a contributing factor in the tragic events of the last twenty years and of the present world catastrophe. Without willing or realizing it, an analysis of the world situation seems indubitably to point to the increasingly determinative influence of America in world relationships. The sooner we recognize this unsought verdict of history, the better it will be for civilization as we have understood and cherished it.

It would be impossible to overstate the effect of these massive social forces upon the American mind and the American way of life. During the past century the orientation and configurations of American culture have undergone great changes. As President Hoover's Commission on Social Trends some years ago pointed out, there has been a considerable shift in the functions of institutions. For some time the family, the church, and the local community have been relinquishing functions to industry and the state. The profile of our culture has greatly changed. There has been phenomenal development in science, technology, and the production of material goods. But there has been a corresponding lag in art, morals, and religion.[9] These results which the commission pointed out appear, perhaps more than in any other way, in the progressive secularization of American life. With the disintegration of the older sanctions of religion the once accepted moral standards have tended to give way before the free expression of undisciplined impulses at the same time that society has lost much of its cohesiveness. One of the marks of a secularized society is its tendency to fall apart in the pursuit of highly specialized and unrelated interests. The great periods of syn-

[9] W. F. Ogburn (ed.), *Recent Social Trends* (New York: McGraw-Hill Book Co., Inc., 1933).

thesis and unity in culture have been periods of religious faith. The supreme task that lies immediately before us is that of redressing the imbalance of our secularized culture by restoring ends to their place of pre-eminence and by subordinating the technical means to their proper relation of relevancy to these ends.

The means for securing the unity of culture have historically been art, philosophy, religion, and great causes, which have kindled the imagination, stirred the emotions, and evoked community of effort. To these must be added in our day the new and growing movement of unified science, which sees life in its interrelatedness. The reason for the effectiveness of religion as an integrative factor seems to lie in the fact that, while art is contemplative and appreciative of life in its wholeness and while philosophy seeks to discover and organize meanings and relations into a consistent system of ideas, religion is concerned with meanings and values in their operational aspect —is concerned fundamentally with the practical issues of living. For this reason unitive science has profound religious implications. For this reason also the totalitarian state has become a religion and is at the present time rightfully recognized as the rival of Christianity and Judaism. When life becomes atomistic, it loses its meaning and a compelling sense of worth. This is a danger to which democracy, with its emphasis upon individualism, is especially subject. There can be little doubt that the recent growing interest in religion springs from a growing dissatisfaction with a type of life that has lost its unity and, therefore, an authentic sense of its reality and worth. Considerations such as these led H. G. Wells to predict that the next great epoch in Western culture would be one of synthesis and, therefore, would be essentially religious.[10] There are indubitable signs that we are already in the opening

[10] *What Shall We Do with Our Lives?* (New York: Doubleday, Doran & Co., 1931).

[18]

phases of that epoch. Some such considerations seem to have effected in Aldous Huxley[11] a change from an attitude of radical cynicism concerning life to an affirmation of life and to his insistence that the time has come for us to re-examine the ends we seek and to restore them to their place of primacy over techniques.

At the moment we are involved in the profoundest way imaginable in the mortal conflict of a global war, fighting in an all-out struggle to preserve the Four Freedoms of mankind against the ruthless aggression of the Axis powers, as well as for the very existence of the nation itself. It takes little imagination to foresee that the effects of the present war upon the American mind will be even more far-reaching than those of World War I. We are being forced to re-examine the democratic ideal for which we are fighting and to extend democracy to the areas where underprivilege still exists in a society of free men. Around this supreme cause the nation has achieved a unity of thought and purpose heretofore undreamed of. In this crisis men are turning to religion for support and security. "There are no atheists in the fox holes of Bataan."

Beyond the winning of the war looms the stupendous task of rebuilding a new world order upon the ruins of the old. The most sensitive observers of the present scene are deeply convinced that America, together with the other nations of the world, stands upon the threshold of a new epoch in history. Our generation is witnessing the death of the old world and the birth of a new world. Destiny stands with us on that threshold while the eternal ages wait to record what that destiny will be. In the present conflict, as President Eduard Beneš[12] has pointed out, the old structures of nationalism throughout the world may be dissolving and the ground may be in process of

[11] *Ends and Means* (New York: Harper & Bros., 1937).

[12] Address before the Quadrangle Club of the University of Chicago. Cf. also Michael Straight, *Make This the Last War* (New York: Harcourt, Brace & Co., 1943).

being cleared for the building of new structures of a just and lasting peace grounded in co-operation and guaranteeing to the common man the conditions of freedom and opportunity and access to the goods of life. Such a task outruns our intellectual habits and our emotional patterns. It is a task which no single nation or group of nations acting alone can accomplish. It will be, if it is achieved, the result of the co-operative thinking and imagination of all the nations, including the vanquished. In this undertaking America, in her new position of responsibility, must play an important role.

That task will require economic and political statesmanship of the highest order. But it will require more than economic and political statesmanship. If we are to achieve a new world of justice, security, and good will, society, as Vice-President Wallace has reminded us, will have to have a new heart. In that undertaking education will play an unprecedented part as the chief social instrument through which the generation that has won the victory and achieved the peace will interpret its values and ideals to the children and young people who will become the citizens of the reborn nation and new world order. Never before has education faced so great an opportunity or so great a responsibility. In the presence of such a responsibility education will need to rethink its nature and social function. Particularly will it need to re-examine itself at the point of its present greatest weakness—at the point of values, ideals, and motivation. Recent history has demonstrated what propagandist education can accomplish in the totalitarian state. It yet remains to be fully demonstrated what a free people in a democratic society can do through education as organized intelligence and values in creating understanding, attitudes, and motives necessary to the free inquiry, high purpose, and sustained effort upon which any democracy must depend. Victory will rest upon a decision of arms. A just and enduring peace will be won, after the diplomatic

[20]

ground has been laid, through a socialized education that is firmly anchored in values.

It is against the background of the interplay of social forces that have shaped American history and that are now, on an unprecedented scale, shaping a planetary society that the problem of religion in education must be considered. Any discussion of the problem in a more restricted context would be superficial, and the conclusions reached would be only palliative. The forms of education which we have inherited have grown up within historical contexts which are forever past and irrecoverable. The precedents which they furnish are not adequate to meet the demands of the present. The new historical situation which the nation faces in a changed world demands the critical re-examination of the ends we seek in education and of the content, method, and organization necessary for their achievement. Certainly we face the demands of the new era as one people bound together in a common destiny, with a total cultural heritage of values as well as techniques and with a total cultural future of spiritual as well as material ideals. It is no advantage to face the future with an education divided by the anachronistic distinction between the secular and the religious. Neither can the traditional alignment of the agencies of society, such as that of church and state, be allowed to obscure the essential nature of the problem or to distort a constructive solution such as the needs of childhood and youth, on the one hand, and of the nation, on the other, demand.

In the chapters that follow we shall consider against this background of the changing American scene the educational situation in America as it has developed as the result of the interaction of the social forces we have reviewed, the fundamental issues involving the nature and ends of education, the functional relation of religion to experience, and the functional relation of church and state, as well as a suggested constructive solution of the problem as it now presents itself.

[21]

II

THE EDUCATIONAL SITUATION
IN AMERICA

THE problem of the relation of religion to education in America is unique. It has nowhere a parallel in any modern nation. It is as indigenous to American culture as is the frontier, the Constitution and the Bill of Rights, or the pragmatic philosophy. It has its roots in the interplay of the social forces that have shaped the American mind and the American way of life. Any attempt to understand it or to solve it must, therefore, be in terms of the concrete social conditions out of which it has arisen and not in terms of abstract educational theory. For the same reason, it can be understood not as an isolated educational or institutional problem but only as a part of the complex tissue of American thought and life.

I

The relation of religion to education must be understood in the wide perspective of the evolution of American culture. Since shortly after the Revolution it has been a problem. But it has never remained the same problem. It has undergone change in each successive period of American history. The form, as well as the urgency, in which it presents itself to our generation is in many repects new. As a consequence, earlier solutions were dated and relevant to then-existing conditions, not conclusive. Like so many problems in a young and dynamic society, it requires fresh examination in the light of emergent conditions and social change. The orientation of the problem in our day is quite different from what it was in the Colonial period, in the days of Thomas Jefferson or Horace Mann, or even at the beginning of this century. In its present form it calls for a different approach and a different solution. Of the urgency of the problem we are increasingly conscious, even if we are less certain concerning the manner in which it may be resolved. In any event, the relation of religion to education under contemporary conditions must be approached in the light of the evolution of the social forces that have shaped American history.

The foundations of the nation were laid in a profoundly religious faith. The European backgrounds of this religious faith were predominantly Protestant, there being only one small Catholic settlement in Maryland. While the motives that led to the first settlement in Virginia and to other settlements in the South were chiefly economic, the southern colonists brought with them their Anglican religious heritage. But for the most part the incentive that led the settlers in the middle and northern colonies to seek their fortunes in the New World was the desire to find religious freedom. This was true also of the French Huguenots who settled in the Carolinas and of the Scotch and Scotch-Irish Presbyterians who settled in the South along the Alleghenies. With the greater number of the first settlers, therefore, religion was not just a formal acceptance of religious traditions and institutions. As a result of persecution in Europe, their loyalty to their inherited religious traditions had been re-examined and transmuted into the most regulative conviction of their lives. By the hazards of their voyage across the Atlantic and the perils and hardships of securing a foothold in the untamed wilderness these convictions were still further deepened. Under the influence of these circumstances the early American mind was shaped into a religious mold. In most of the colonies religion was the first concern of life.

As a consequence, the earliest education in America was

predominantly religious. In the middle and northern colonies it was under the control of the church. In the southern colonies charity schools, sponsored by the English Society for the Propagation of the Gospel in Foreign Parts and designed for the poorer communicants of the English national church, taught, in addition to reading, writing, and some arithmetic, the catechism and the religious observances of the Anglican church.

Within this general framework, however, there was great diversity in the population, social structure, and religious life among the colonies. The northern colonies were settled almost wholly by Calvinistic English Puritans, who brought with them a theocratic conception of society. In this homogeneous group, church and state were united. While the schools were largely patterned on English models, laws were early enacted requiring communities to provide schools at public expense for all the young. These schools were religious in content, spirit, and administration. The curriculum consisted of the hornbook, containing the Lord's Prayer from which the alphabet was learned; the Bible; and the catechism. Teachers were selected for their orthodoxy and piety, and the supervision of the schools was in the hands of the clergy. The state executed the ideals and purposes of the church.

The middle colonies, on the other hand, were heterogeneous. They were settled by Dutch Calvinists, Anglicans, Presbyterians, German Lutherans, Swedish Lutherans, Baptists, and Quakers. With these competing sects there could be no union of church and state. Education assumed the parochial pattern, in which the several sects assumed all responsibility for education in complete independence of the state.

In the southern colonies the Anglican church remained the established church. The state assumed no responsibility for education, and the church assumed little more. The physical character of the region gave rise to an agrarian economy of the plantation type, with wealthy landowners, indentured white servants, and Negro slaves. Under these conditions a class society developed in contrast with the democratic society of the New England colonies. Within such a social structure the education of the aristocratic landowning class followed closely the English model, with tutorial instruction in the home, instruction in private select schools, or education in England. The education of the poor was confined to a system of apprenticeship and a few pauper schools. There could be no common schools as in New England.

This negative attitude of church and state toward education in the southern colonies accounts for the relatively slow development of education as a public function in the South— an attitude that for a long time characterized the regions westward to which the southern colonists migrated. In contrast, the concern of a united church and state for education in New England accounts for the relatively rapid development of universal and compulsory education in the North. It was from this highly developed educational consciousness and the provisions that grew out of it, particularly in Massachusetts, that the major educational impulse spread westward with the development of the frontier into the North and the Middle West and became responsible for the general educational pattern of the United States. In the middle colonies, where the competing churches had no instrument in the state for universalizing their educational ideals, the parochial system remained relatively static and contributed little to the development of education in the nation.

II

However, with the development of national life, American education underwent profound changes. Of these, one of the most significant was the secularization of education—a process that was ultimately to result in the exclusion of religion from the public school. Such a result is best understood, not as an event, but as a process. In a process so complex and involving the interplay of so many social forces, it is difficult definitely to fix its beginning or to determine when it was completed. It may be said, however, that by 1800 secularization was well under way and that it reached its consummation three-quarters of a century later when, by 1875, the general pattern of state constitutional revisions or enactments in regard to education was quite definitely established.

There were many factors that entered into the secularization of American education. Undoubtedly, one of the foremost among them was the growth of the frontier. In New England, which was most extensively to influence American education, the civil and religious unit was the town, with its democratic town meeting and with the church and school as the focal centers of the community. But as the population moved into the unoccupied lands new communities sprang up too remote by natural barriers or distance to permit attendance at the town meeting-house or the school. A new geographical factor entered into the onetime compact community with its natural boundaries. The outgrowth of the operation of this factor was the autonomous school district, with its own school, its own taxing system, and its own supervision. With the ever expanding frontier the district system became the prevailing unit of education in the Northwest and the Middle West and even extended into the South. It was an intermediate state between the homogeneous New England town and the state systems of American education. The school district was predominantly a civil, rather than a religious, unit.

The geographical factor was, however, only one of the transforming influences of the expanding frontier. With the ever westward movement of the frontier across the Appalachians, the plains, and the western prairies, new functions arose and with them new structures of national life. Agriculture on a wide scale and the growth of cities with their industries gave rise to commerce, communication, surveying, and transportation. With the winning of independence and the formation of a national organization, governmental functions arose, with their legislative, judicial, and administrative activities. These emerging functions placed new demands upon education for an intelligent citizenship and for the equipment of all the people with the new knowledge and skills necessary for participating in a common national life. For these functions the meager Colonial education in all but exclusively religious subjects no longer sufficed. Neither, with the rise of states carved out of the wilderness and inhabited by large communities, could these growing demands upon education be met by local communities. It was inevitable that education should become the responsibility of the states, with power to levy taxes and to exercise supervision. In this way the ground was laid for education as a national responsibility, the full implications of which have only recently been grasped. Inevitable as state control of education was, it was only after a long and bitter struggle with private religious agencies and local school districts that that shift was completely made.

In the meantime a vast and growing tide of immigration had set in. By 1880, of a population of 50,155,783, 13.3 per cent were foreign-born. While most of these were from northern European countries, a considerable and growing stream came from central, eastern, and southern Europe —a tide that was greatly to change the character of the earlier immigrant stock. In this way the heterogeneity of the American population was greatly increased, not only in racial stock but in cultural, political, and religious backgrounds. Thus, increasingly, a new burden was laid upon education in assimilating these divergent population elements and in preparing their children for citizenship. This, too, was a result of the expanding frontier, with its unoccupied land, its growing industry, and its unlimited opportunity.

[27]

To these factors must be added a growing secularization of American culture. Its general orientation was less and less toward the deeply religious values that were cherished by the colonists and more and more toward a preoccupation with immediate temporal activities, the accumulation of wealth, and "success."

But undoubtedly the most immediately effective factor in the exclusion of religion from the public schools was the sectarianism of religion in America. The churches were extremely reluctant to relinquish their hold on the schools. The issue was brought to a decisive crisis by the insistence of the churches upon a division of educational funds. Acute as was the rivalry among the Protestant sects, it was further accentuated by the increase of Catholic immigration. After a long and bitter struggle, led chiefly by Horace Mann in Massachusetts, the tension was resolved by amendments to state constitutions and by enactments in the constitutions of newly admitted states, beginning in 1848 with Wisconsin's forbidding the division of public funds with sectarian schools and prohibiting the teaching of sectarian religion in the public schools. This attitude was quite definitely established by 1875. It resulted in fixing firmly the now universally accepted principle of the separation of church and state. The secularization of public education was complete.

III

(The result of this historical development was a complete split in the program and organization of American education. As a consequence, the state assumed responsibility for the cultural, scientific, civic, and technological education of the nation's childhood and youth as a public function, while the churches found themselves faced with the responsibility of providing such education in religion as they could under the limitations which circumstances placed upon them. That this was a solution of an intolerable problem during the early and middle nineteenth century—perhaps, in the light of the conditions of the period, the inevitable solution—no one can doubt. Neither can one doubt that there were invaluable constructive and enduring elements in the solution. This was especially true of the establishment of religious tolerance, the safeguarding of the rights of minority groups, and the establishment of the principle of a free church in a free society. Neither can there be any doubt that this solution freed the schools to go forward in the development of one of the most effective programs of education in the civilized world.

But that, in the light of subsequent history, it was a satisfactory or permanent solution we who are approaching the middle of the twentieth century are increasingly doubtful. The practical outcomes of the solution could not be foreseen, nor was it possible to take into account all the factors in a situation that was to undergo unpredictable development. It begins to be clear that it has bequeathed to our generation a problem more complex and more difficult than the original one. Many of the consequences of the earlier "solution" were not contemplated or intended. An examination of the legislation clearly shows that it was the exclusion of *sectarian* religious teaching that was intended and not the exclusion of religion itself. It was the view of Horace Mann that the Bible was an invaluable book for forming the character of children and that it should be read without comment in the schools. S. W. Brown seems quite objectively to sum up the situation when he says:

Differences of religious belief and a sound regard on the part of the State for individual freedom in religious matters, coupled with the necessity for centralization and uniformity, rather than hostility to religion as such lie at the bottom of the movement toward the secular school.[1]

Only subsequent events could bring the hidden factors to the surface. Now we begin to see them in their stark and disturbing outlines.

[1] Quoted by E. P. Cubberley in *Public Education in the United States* (Boston: Houghton Mifflin Co., 1919), p. 173.

The changes of the past half-century, not only in the life of the nation but in our conception of the functional relation of religion to personal and social experience and in our understanding of the nature and ends of education itself, require that the problem shall be re-examined in the light of both the contemporary American and the international situation. It becomes the more easy to do this when we think of American culture in terms of a dynamic process in which continuity and change are inseparably united. It then becomes possible to appraise the earlier solution in relation to its relevant historical context rather than as a final and static solution in a changed and changing social situation.

Before we examine the reactions of both the churches and the schools to the situation created by the exclusion of religion from the schools, it will be well to examine the unintended consequences of this decision that were not then foreseen but which now begin to assume major importance both for the children and youth of the nation and for the nation itself.

Perhaps the most obvious of these results has been the distortion of the cultural inheritance of children and young people. On any account, public education as a social function is the most authentic interpreter of a people's culture. As the history of education from primitive times unequivocally shows, education is the conscious and intentional attempt of a people to interpret and transmit to its young the operative values that it most deeply cherishes and upon which it depends for the perpetuation and extension of its life in the future.

Now, from every point of view, religion is one of the fundamental component elements of the cultural history of mankind. It is, in the view of one of the most astute students of social history, man's oldest and most fundamental reaction to his world.[2] It is impossible for the anthropologist to give a descriptive account of the most primitive societies without giv-

[2] Franklin H. Giddings, in an unpublished lecture.

ing a large place to religious beliefs and practices. On the basis of anthropological and historical as well as psychological data Edward Scribner Ames identifies religion as the heightening and idealization of social values.[3] Émile Durkheim, from the point of view of a social psychologist, advances the thesis that, when religion and social organization are traced back to their elementary forms, they merge in totemism as the objectification and symbolization of the essential communal life of the group.[4] George A. Coe, approaching religion from the standpoint of psychology, identifies religion as the revaluation of all particular values that are operative in the group life.[5] In his portrayal of the structure of the human mind, William H. Sheldon employs a scheme of five "panels"— of material relations, of social dominance and submission, of sexual relations, of orientation, and of feeling-awareness.[6] Of these essential aspects of the whole person's interaction with his objective world, the fourth panel—that of orientation—is concerned with religious attitudes. These views are indicative of the unmistakable trend in the scientific understanding of religion for more than half a century.

Certainly it would be impossible to give an account of man's intellectual history without including his reflections upon his experience in terms of origins, destiny, the nature of his own existence, and the nature of reality, as recorded in his philosophical and theological speculations. The vast theological libraries are at the same time a witness of the importance of these issues to his insatiable curiosity and a record of his evolving insights into the ends and meaning of life.

No more would it be possible to write the history of social

[3] *The Psychology of Religious Experience* (Boston: Houghton Mifflin Co., 1910), p. 280 and *passim*.

[4] *Les Formes élémentaires de la vie religieuse* (Paris: F. Alcan, 1912).

[5] *The Psychology of Religion* (Chicago: University of Chicago Press, 1916).

[6] *Psychology and the Promethean Will* (New York: Harper & Bros., 1936).

institutions in the Western world without taking full account of the church and its allied organizations. Religion involves large-scale social behaviors that find expression in institutions and mores. During the long period of the Middle Ages the church was the dominant social institution and the cohesive social influence that held society together. There can be no pretense of adequacy in a social analysis of the modern community that leaves out organized religion. The operations of religion are under way in every American community, involving approximately half the population of the nation, imposing buildings, large budgets, many types of religious organizations, and a wide variety of religious activities.

Similarly, it is quite impossible to understand the art and literature of the Western world apart from religion. Religion has furnished the motif for a large part of painting, sculpture, architecture, and music. It would be difficult to overestimate the influence which the Bible and the Hebrew-Christian faith have had upon the moral and intellectual outlook, the social behaviors, and the institutional structures of Western civilization in general and of American life in particular. Over the centuries the influence of religion has been comparable with that of science, technology, and politics.

By the exclusion of religion from public education as the most authentic interpreter of our cultural past or of the American way of life the cultural inheritance of the nation's children and youth has been not only distorted but dismembered and falsified. Its children and young people are denied that part of their rightful tradition wherein is rooted "faith in an ordered universe and the fatherhood of God."

But, if the cultural inheritance of the child is dismembered, so also is the child. By failing to deal with the deeper valuational attitudes of the child's experience, education fails to deal with the whole child and with the orientation of his whole self toward reality. It leaves unmet the profoundest needs of his nature as a human being. This is particularly true of life in the modern world as contrasted with life among primitive peoples or in the great periods of cultural unity, as Dr. C. G. Jung has pointed out.

Modern man has suffered an almost fatal shock, and as a result has fallen into profound uncertainty. . . . . The modern man has lost all the metaphysical certainties of his mediaeval brother, and set up in their place ideals of material security, general welfare and humaneness. . . . . Science has destroyed even the refuge of the inner life. What was once a sheltering haven has become a place of terror. . . . . It is no wonder, then, in my opinion, if the modern man falls back upon the reality of psychic life and expects from it that certainty which the world denies him. . . . . What we actually see is that the Western world strikes up a still more rapid tempo—the American tempo—the very opposite of quietism and resigned aloofness. An enormous tension arises between the opposite poles of outer and inner life, between objective and subjective reality. Perhaps it is a final race between ageing Europe and young America. . . . . A psycho-neurosis must be understood as the suffering of a human being who has not discovered what life means for him. . . . . Human thought cannot conceive any system or final truth that could give the patient help in order to live: that is faith, hope, love and insight. . . . . Among all my patients in the second half of life—that is to say, over thirty-five—there has not been one whose problem in the last resort was not that of finding a religious outlook on life.[7]

These tensions of modern life are accentuated by the fact that in the church and in the religious home the growing person is led to believe that religion is the most important concern of life, while in the school religion is relegated to a position of unimportance by being treated with silence or neglect. The result is more serious than appears on the surface. Without intending it, the school is placed in a position of exerting a negative influence regarding religion, since what appears to be neutrality turns out practically to be a discrediting of religion. It is equally tragic that under these conditions the resources of religion for personal counseling are rendered for the most part unavailable in the school. This constitutes a particularly serious problem in the light of Dr. Jung's observation quoted above.

[7] *Modern Man in Search of a Soul* (New York: Harcourt, Brace & Co., 1933), pp. 231, 235, 236, 245, 254.

Furthermore, it turns out that under the present arrangement less than half of the children and young people five to seventeen years of age are receiving any systematic religious training, whether Protestant, Catholic, or Jewish. The longtime cumulative consequences of this situation are not difficult to foresee. Education under church auspices turns out to be religious education for the youth constituencies of the several denominations or major faiths, with the vast interstices of the population almost wholly neglected. It is not a sufficient answer to say that these masses are cared for by such character education as is provided in the public schools. Aside from limitations in the number and programs of schools that are giving character education, it yet remains to be demonstrated that any program of character education can be wholly effective that does not in one way or another take religious attitudes and commitments into account. Both psychology and history raise grave doubts as to whether a purely secular ethics can support the moral life under the stresses of the modern world.

It is not, however, the needs of children and young people alone that are involved. American democracy has a stake in the solution of this problem. Monarchies find their sources of unity largely in the emotionally charged symbols of the crown or the person of his royal majesty. The totalitarian state finds its unity in the unlimited authority of a dictator and in the erection of the state, as an object of loyalty, into the position of the supreme value that transcends and regulates all other values, under such slogans as "blood and soil," "a new order for Asia," or the supremacy of a ruling class. Democracy, on the other hand, is an association of free individuals in a community of shared values and responsibilities. Its cohesion depends upon loyalty to a common body of ideals and purposes that are capable of stirring the emotions, kindling the imagination, and evoking sustained effort in the achievement of common ends. While religion cannot be identified with democ-

[34]

racy, the roots of modern democracy are deeply imbedded in the Hebrew-Christian religion, with its emphasis upon the worth of persons, the dominance of community over race and class, the fatherhood of God, and the brotherhood of man. Reciprocally, democracy is essential to free and vital religion. At the moment the most deadly rival of Christianity and Judaism is the religion of the totalitarian state, with its emphasis on race and class and the use of unmitigated force. Democracy can scarcely hope to compete with these aggressive forms of totalitarianism unless it can evoke wholehearted commitments to the Four Freedoms that are essential to the good life for the common man. In the judgment of many, these values are in their deepest nature profoundly religious and Christian in their implications. In these fundamental and comprehending values of the good life for all lie at once the cohesive force of the democratic state and its dynamic. It is upon such values as these that a new world order will have to be erected when the decision of arms makes the winning of the peace possible, if such a world order is to be just and enduring.

IV

The reactions of both churches and schools to the situation created by the exclusion of religion have been varied. The oldest reaction of certain communions, notably the Catholic and the Lutheran, followed the pattern of the parochial school already established in the middle colonies. According to this plan, the churches assume all responsibility for the total education of the young of their respective constituencies. This they do at their own expense while submitting to taxation by the state for public education. That this policy, if universalized, is not a solution of the educational needs of the nation few would seriously question. Whatever other weaknesses parochial education may have, from the point of view of modern educational theory and practice, it cannot be said to meet the requirements of a democracy that rests upon a community of shared educational experiences rather than upon the segregated experience of a class or sect. Moreover, even for the communions that have adopted this system it is not proving adequate. Only one-half of the Catholic children of elementary age and one-fourth of the Catholic young people of high-school age are in Catholic schools.[8] The Presbyterians, after a brief and unsatisfactory experiment in this direction, abandoned the proposal.[9] For a time, in communities that were wholly or almost wholly Catholic, Catholic instruction was offered under the control of the public school, and the schools in these instances were designated as Catholic public schools. This practice, however, has not proved satisfactory and has, for the most part, been discontinued.[10] Supplementing the work of the parochial schools, the Catholics, through the Confraternity of Christian Doctrine, have provided Catholic instruction in Sunday schools, weekday schools, and vacation schools.[11]

The Protestant churches turned to the Sunday school, which had been imported from England toward the end of the eighteenth century. The Sunday school was one phase of the philanthropic movement in education in Europe. It had its origin in social conditions very different from those prevailing in America, being designed to meet the needs of urchins on the streets of Gloucester. Its efforts were devoted to the moral rehabilitation of this underprivileged group and to teaching the three R's and some elements of religion. After its adoption by the Protestant churches its motivation, until the beginning of the present century, remained for the most part philanthropic

[8] Roy G. Deferrari (ed.), *Essays on Catholic Education in the United States* (Washington, D.C.: Catholic University of America Press, 1942), pp. 459 and 465.

[9] Lewis J. Sherrill, *Presbyterian Parochial Schools: 1846–1870* (New Haven, Conn.: Yale University Press, 1932).

[10] Deferrari, *op. cit.*, pp. 30 ff.

[11] *Ibid.*, pp. 447 ff.

[36]

and evangelistic rather than educational. Like the parochial school, its services are limited almost exclusively to the children and youth of the respective denominations, leaving untouched the great areas of child and youth population not affiliated with the several churches.

Since the beginning of the century great strides have been made in educationalizing the work of the Sunday schools, now generally known as Sunday church schools. The educational efforts of the Protestant churches during the last twenty years have been consolidated through the International Council of Religious Education, representing forty-one denominations and approximately 85 per cent of the Protestants of the United States and Canada. Protestant churches co-operating through the International Council have formulated a progressive policy of religious education and have worked out standards and programs in keeping with the best educational theory and practice.[12] However, at its best the Sunday school is forced to do its work under narrow limitations of time, with lay teachers under the supervision of a small professional group, and with totally inadequate financial support.

Recognition of these limitations in the functioning of the Sunday school has led the Protestant churches to extend their educational program to weekday sessions and to the summer vacation period. The weekday church school, first undertaken in Gary, Indiana, upon the invitation of Superintendent Wirt in 1914, is held on time released from the public school schedule at the request of parents or in afterschool hours. Usually the sessions are held in church buildings, and the children and young people are taught by teachers supplied by the churches, under church supervision and support. In some instances the instruction is given by the several denominations to the children of their own constituencies. The predominant

[12] Cf. *Christian Education Today* (Chicago: International Council of Religious Education, 1942).

trend has been to offer weekday religious instruction co-operatively under the supervision of an interdenominational council in the community. In some instances such religious instruction is given in public school property by teachers provided by the churches. In a smaller number of cases religious instruction is given in the public schools by teachers certified by the state, but at church expense.

The Protestant weekday school has grown to national proportions, having extended to most of the states and most of the principal metropolitan centers. Quite recently it has been extended to the high-school level, with or without credit. When offered for credit, religious instruction is included in the group of electives. In the last five years new attention has been directed toward this plan, the initiative being taken by an increasing number of public school authorities.

The significance of weekday religious education lies in the fact that it is an attempt to relate religious education to public education. Its success has varied with different communities. In some cases, through the use of this arrangement by Protestants, Catholics, and Jews, a high percentage of the school enrolment has been reached. The general trend of experience seems to demonstrate that the plan leads to tolerance, understanding, and co-operation among the adherents of the several religious faiths. In many instances the teachers and supervisors are professionally trained, with compensation comparable with that of the corresponding grades in the public schools. An attempt has been made to correlate the work of religious instruction with instruction in the public schools. That it is a solution of the basic problem perhaps none of its most ardent advocates would affirm. But it does afford a considerable body of experience that may well prove useful in searching for a more fundamental and satisfactory solution.

The Jews, in attempting to meet the problem of the exclusion of religion from public education, have placed their main dependence upon a school of religion meeting in afterschool hours for one hour each day in three or four shifts, so that the Jewish child receives from five to seven and one-half hours of religious instruction each week. In these schools the Hebrew Bible is studied in Hebrew, with supplementary study of the fundamentals of religion and the history of Judaism. These schools range from the kindergarten or the second grade through the high school. They reach approximately 40 per cent of the Jewish children and young people. They vary with localities both in time and in placement of emphasis in their instruction. There is a definite trend toward dealing with the contemporary experiences of Jewish children and young people. Teachers and supervisors are professionally trained and are compensated comparably with teachers in the corresponding grades of the public school.

The Jews supplement the work of their weekday schools with religious instruction in Sunday schools. The subject matter of the Jewish Sunday school consists of the study of the Bible and other religious literature in English, the fundamentals of religion, Jewish history, and Jewish observances. The work of these schools is correlated with that in the weekday schools. The Jewish Sunday school reaches approximately 60 per cent of the children and youth of Judaism. Above these levels the Jews also provide advanced religious instruction in the College of Jewish Education which reaches a relatively small number of Jewish youth.

Reaction to this problem, however, has not been limited to the churches. A small number of public schools have recently included religion as an integral part of their programs on the same basis as language, general science, literature, history, civics, and the arts; it is taught by public school teachers, under public school supervision, for credit, and on public funds. As the superintendent of an important midwest system expressed it, the greatest weakness of public education is at the point of ideals and motivation. The sectarianism of the churches in his community, together with their educational inexperience, led him to propose this course to his board. Manifestly, this reaction on the part of public schools, as yet very limited in extent, grows out of the conviction that a public system of education is unsatisfactory if such a system is designed for all the people and is committed to meeting the needs of childhood and youth as well as to interpreting the American way of life but neglects the religious needs of the child and the religious aspects of culture .

While the problem has thus far been discussed for the most part from the viewpoint of elementary and secondary education, it is quite as much a problem of higher education. The earliest colleges in America were religious foundations. As late as 1860, of the 246 colleges only 17 were state institutions. Even now, of the 1,690 institutions of higher learning in the United States most of the 1,090 privately controlled were founded and are now operated by the churches. But with the rapid rise of the modern public high school, the junior college, and the state university the public system of education is complete from the elementary grades to the professional school. Aside from the increasingly unpredictable future of church-related colleges, by far the greater number of church young people attend state institutions. The same basic considerations pertain to state teachers colleges and state universities that pertain to elementary and secondary education. For some time courses in religion have been included as an integral part of the programs of some of these state institutions. Certain state teachers colleges are contemplating making training in religion a basic and required part of the professional preparation for the state certification of teachers.

III

FUNDAMENTAL ASSUMPTIONS

IN THE growing concern of churchmen, educators, and citizens regarding the situation created by the exclusion of religion from public education, there are a meeting of minds and an increasingly urgent conviction that a solution must be found. There is also a fund of experience upon which to draw for guidance. But before any constructive solution for the present educational situation can be proposed, certain fundamental assumptions need to be re-examined in the light of changes that are taking place in our thinking about the basic issues that underlie the problem. These assumptions have to do with the nature and ends of education as a social responsibility, the nature and function of religion, and the relation of church and state.

I

Perhaps in no aspect of our common life have there been greater changes than in the way we have come to think of the nature and ends of education. We came to the beginning of the century with an inheritance of notions about education that grew up out of older forms of social living and a different orientation of culture. While we have been experimenting with a democratic way of life, we have depended for the most part upon forms of education that are traditional, external, and authoritative.

Roughly speaking, these traditional notions of education lived on in a flowing-together of three conceptions of education that, though they had different cultural origins, were in many respects congruous. As a result, educational theory and practice represent a kind of syncretism of unanalyzed assumptions which, like philosophy and theology until quite recently, were on the whole rationalizations of the operative but uncriticized values of older social forms.

Perhaps the oldest of these notions was a conception of education as social discipline. That idea of education is as old as education itself, going back to the most primitive societies. As Agnes De Lima some years ago pointed out, organized adult society has always been conscious of a tension between the fresh and spontaneous interests and activities of its young and the established forms of organized and sanctioned social behavior.[1] Therefore, the purpose of education has always tended to be thought of in terms of the repression of the spontaneous behavior of the young and the molding of them into the going thought-forms, institutions, and habits of society.

Though this notion of education is very old, it received philosophical formulation chiefly by John Locke in the seventeenth century. The occasion for this rationalization of disciplinary education was the rise of the scientific and romantic movements that stemmed from the Renaissance. The earliest enthusiasm of the Renaissance educators was for the classics as the subject matter of education. But as interest in the phenomena and processes of the natural world grew and attention shifted to the inner emotions of the common man, the concerns of the immediately present world and the use of the vernacular threatened the traditional classical education. Therefore the defense of the classics on the ground that formal subjects, especially the classical languages, afforded the best discipline for the mind, then thought to be composed of faculties. In this way disciplinary education achieved intellectual respectability and fastened itself upon education until the end of the nineteenth century. As a result of its influence, the content of education was extremely narrow, being limited almost entirely to Greek, Latin, and mathematics, with grudging recognition of such subjects as history, the natural sciences, and

[1] *Our Enemy the Child* (New York: New Republic, Inc., 1926).

the social sciences; and it was wholly prescribed. President Wilson, before he relinquished the presidency of Princeton to become president of the United States, affirmed that the purpose of education was to sharpen one's mind as an ax is sharpened. The basic method in this type of education was training through habit formation.

The idea of education as the transmission of knowledge is also as old as education itself. However, as a result of the discoveries of science and the mountainous accumulation of valuable knowledge, the concept of education as the transmission of knowledge was immensely accentuated and assumed modern form. The new content subjects began to find their way into the curriculum—physics, chemistry, biology, economics, sociology, and the practical arts. As it became impossible for anyone to master more than a segment of existing knowledge, prescription gave way to the free election of subjects, as at Harvard and the University of Michigan. Out of the resulting chaos arose the organization of majors and minors, or groupings of electives, with specialization in particular fields of knowledge. As late as the beginning of the century, President Nicholas M. Butler defined education as the gradual adjustment of the young to the great traditions of culture literary, historical, scientific, aesthetic, technological, and religious.[2] The method of this type of education was instruction as formulated in the "five formal steps" by Herbart. Undoubtedly, in spite of recent advances in educational theory, this continues to be the dominant mode of education in America.

The first break from these older and more external notions of education occurred in the late nineteenth century in the form of the conception of education as recapitulation, as formulated in this country chiefly by President G. Stanley Hall. It grew out of the doctrine of evolution and was predicated upon the idea that the child in his prenatal life repeated the

[2] *The Meaning of Education* (New York: Macmillan Co., 1907).

biological history of his subhuman ancestry and that subsequent to his birth he rehearsed in his own experience the great epochs of culture. The emphasis was thereby shifted from discipline and the transmission of knowledge to inner growth through the unfolding of innate impulses predetermined by biological heredity. The method of this notion of education was the presentation in proper sequence and at the appropriate time of the products of the culture epochs. This idea, along with the influence of Froebel and Pestalozzi, focused attention upon persons and growth, though as a mode of education it had an enthusiastic but short-lived vogue.

These notions of education—as discipline, the transmission of knowledge, and inner growth—furnished the component elements which, without analysis or criticism, formed the conglomerate that was American education at the beginning of the twentieth century. In its content it was dominated by tradition, and in its method it was external, formal, and authoritative. Being backward-looking, it was preoccupied with the precedents of the past rather than with the creative and releasing possibilities of contemporary experience. Evidence of tension and dissatisfaction with the traditional forms of education began to appear in a literature of criticism that had its rise around the beginning of the century with the writings of John Dewey, directed at philosophical, psychological, and social inconsistencies in then-existing American education. Slow in its beginning, by the time of World War I this literature had reached a considerable volume. By 1925 the fundamental issues had been brought forward and debated and the present trends in theory and practice were well established, at least in those areas of education that are sensitive to intellectual and social change.

As a result of these changes in point of view, it now begins to be clear that the function of education as a social responsibility in a democracy is not merely to transmit the end-products of historical culture as such, or to mold the young into inherited thought-forms and institutions, or merely to unfold the "innate" characteristics of individual persons. Instead, it begins to be clear that the function of education in a democracy is to assist the young in dealing intelligently and effectively with the issues of contemporary life with the aid of the resources of the funded experience of the past as that experience is recorded in the great traditions. Equally it is the function of education in a democracy to assist its future citizens in acquiring those methods of thought and those attitudes of co-operation and self-discipline upon which responsible participation in a democracy rests. Education for a democracy must develop initiative, competence in dealing with the issues of the common life through critical analysis of factors and outcomes, and ability to make decisions and carry them through into action.

Translated into practice, this means that education begins with the actual experience of living persons where they are in their interaction with their real and present world. Its content consists of units of experience, set in the context of a dynamic and changing culture, as these experiences arise out of the manifold relations of personal and social living. The subject matter of science, history, literature, and the arts is relevant to these experiences as resources for interpreting, analyzing, judging, and bringing them through in the completed act. Education so conceived is creative—an achievement on the part of free persons. The burden of education shifts from teaching to learning and from passive assimilation of tradition to inquiry, commitment, and constructive action.

If, as is now understood, persons become the kind of persons they do become neither through the unfolding of "innate" tendencies nor through the external pressures of the environing world but rather through the interaction of the growing person with his objective world of nature, society, and culture, then the process of education as heretofore understood is greatly altered and extended. It overruns the boundaries of any given institution, be it the school, the family, or the church. Its focus shifts to the community where experiences are being had if, when, and as they arise in the school, in the family, in the church, on the playground, in vocation, at the movies, and especially through participation in various groups in which a role is assumed or assigned.

Such considerations as these would seem to indicate that the base of the education of the whole person needs to be extended beyond the formal classroom to include the organization of the whole range of relations and of the experiences that arise from them. They make education a function of the whole society. This seems to call for the co-operation of all the agencies in the community that in one way or another affect the growth of children and young people. All these agencies need to sit down before the needs of children and young people and ask what contributions they have to make to the total education of the whole person in relation to the democratic community.

Such considerations as these also carry far-reaching implications for society itself. When, from this functional and creative point of view, adult society sets out to educate its young in terms of the living issues of contemporary American life, it finds that it is under the necessity of educating itself. In view of the fact that the arrangements of existing society are in the control of adults, who alone have power to change them, it begins to be evident that we cannot have a better education for our young until we have a better adult society. This insight has led not a few educators to the conviction that the most crucial point at which to attack education for a democracy is at the adult level, without, of course, lessening what is being done for the education of children and young people.

II

Not less significant are the changes that are beginning to appear in the manner of conceiving the nature and function of religion as the result of the scientific study of religion during the last half-century. In the early period of our national life, and still predominantly, religion was understood chiefly in terms of theology, ceremonial, and the ecclesiastical institution. Its theological doctrines were regarded as having been supernaturally revealed in the Bible as an authoritative book. Its sacraments were regarded as the almost exclusive channels of divine grace. The church was thought of as a sacramental institution of uniquely divine origin, independent of, if not in opposition to, secular society. There were, and still are, wide cleavages between Protestant, Catholic, and Jewish faiths. Protestantism, because of its radical individualism, has been divided into a multitude of more or less antagonistic and competing sects. The latest census shows more than two hundred of these religious sects in America. As we have seen, it was this sectarianism of religion in America that caused the exclusion of religion from public education, and not religion as such. It would appear perfectly obvious that there is at the present time no more hope of public education's including sectarian religion than there was at the time when in the interests of the public good it was originally excluded. Unless religion can be dissociated from its sectarian elements, there would appear to be no hope of solving the present dilemma.

Fortunately, however, as was pointed out in chapter i, as a result of the anthropological, ethnological, historical, psychological, and sociological methods a new approach to the understanding of religion is taking form. Its result is a functional conception of religion. When subjected to the methods of these sciences, religious behavior is seen to be as amenable to observation, analysis, and redirection as any other form of human behavior. Under objective analysis it appears as a phase of a people's total culture. As such, it differs in its forms of expression from one culture group to another. This is true not only of national groups, such as Egypt as compared with Babylonia or Greece as compared with Palestine, but also of cultural areas within our own nation, such as New England as compared with the Middle West or with the Deep South. As Professor Richard Niebuhr has pointed out, the types of religion in America follow closely the social stratifications of the population.[3] Speaking broadly, the major denominations stem from economic and cultural differences as well as from theological differences.

It is equally significant that religious beliefs and practices of the same social group change as the culture of the group changes. For this reason it is impossible to speak of "the religion" of the Jews or of Christianity except in the most general and abstract terms. One must, on the contrary, speak of the Jewish religion as of specific periods, such as the nomadic period, the period of migration and conquest, the period of settlement upon the land and nation-building, the period of international involvement, or the period of national decline. So, also, one must speak of the Christianity of New Testament times, the Christianity of the patristic period, medieval Christianity, the Christianity of the Reformation, or contemporary Christianity. During these periods Judaism and Christianity have undergone profound changes in the content of their beliefs and in their institutional structures. All religions are historical and social processes in which continuity and change are indissolubly united. These changes have always taken place in relation to changes in the environing culture or within the movement itself. At no time in history have these changes in religion been in greater evidence than in contemporary America.

[3] *The Social Sources of Denominationalism* (New York: Henry Holt & Co., 1929).

This is true, as the scientific students of religion have come to believe, because religion sustains a functional relation to the evolving experience of the common life, comparable to the functional relations sustained to culture by science, technology, the arts, and various social institutions such as the family and the state. Religion is a phase of a people's total interaction with the objective world of nature, organized society, and the accumulated traditions of the historic past. At the level of such interaction religion is a quality that is diffused throughout every dimension of a people's practical interests and activities. It is an orientation toward life as a whole. Specifically, it falls within a people's valuational attitudes and occurs when all particular and specialized values are fused into a total meaning and worth of life. While religion has profound personal implications, it is essentially a socially shared experience.

Religion, therefore, sustains a twofold and reciprocal functional relation to the total experience of a people. On the one hand, it appears when all the varied specialized interests and activities of a people—economic, intellectual, political, aesthetic, and moral—are integrated and idealized in terms of fundamental and comprehending values. Thus a religious value is always some other kind of value. But it is in its essential quality different from any other kind of value or from the mere sum of all other values. Its distinctive quality lies in the revaluation of all other values in relation to ultimate reality. On the other hand, once this integration of values has been achieved, religion reacts upon each particular interest and activity as a factor of reconstruction. This it does by subjecting each social process—economic, intellectual, political, aesthetic, and moral —to the radical cross-criticism of all other values. The tendency, especially of a highly advanced culture, is for each specialized activity to become dissociated from the whole and to be pursued intensely as an end in itself. Religion insists that it shall be brought under the judgment of all other values and especially that it shall be appraised in the searching light of that organization of fundamental and comprehending values which the religious mind associates with the idea of God. This is why religion in its prophetic and creative moments assumes the role of critic and seeks the reconstruction of social processes that neglect or destroy these fundamental values, and thus becomes an influence of social reformation. It envisions a new and ideal organization of the common life as the Kingdom of God. This passion burned in the hearts of the eighth-century prophets and in the heart of Jesus. It is the inspiring hope of the modern social gospel.

The integrative function of religion explains how the specific changing content and form of changing religious concepts, practices, and institutions derive from the changing practical interests and activities of the social group. In the history of religion there is no more striking illustration of this relation than in the development of the concept of God in the Jewish religion in relation to the evolution of their economic, social, political, and intellectual life. During the nomadic period of the primitive Hebrew clansmen, with a pastoral economy, they thought of Yahweh as a tribal deity, moving with the tribe from pasture land to pasture land. During the period of migration and conquest their culture became militaristic, and Yahweh became to them Yahweh of Hosts, a conquering deity giving them victory in battle and commanding the annihilation or enslavement of the conquered. During the period of settlement upon the land their economy became agricultural, and Yahweh assumed the functions of the Baalistic deities of the Amorites and became Lawgiver to the emerging theocratic state. It was not until the Hebrew nation was lifted out of its isolation in Palestine and thrust into the theater of international conflict between the world powers of Egypt on the south and Assyria on the north that ethical monotheism emerged from its primitive forms and Yahweh became universalized, spiritualized, and ethicized, Nor was it until the political structures of the Hebrew nation were dissolved and the Temple was destroyed that individualism appeared in Hebrew religion and the individual person stood in immediate and responsible relation to God.

In a similar way it is possible to trace the development of the fundamental concepts of Christian theology in relation to cultural change, as in the case of the doctrine of the person of Christ, the nature of man, sin, the atonement, the eucharist, and the church. With penetrating insight Dean Shailer Mathews traced the evolution of the doctrine of the atonement in relation to the changes in the political structures of Europe.[4] The massive metaphysical theology of the Roman Catholic church cannot be understood except in relation to the context of medieval society. Neither is it possible to understand the current reaction of neo-orthodoxy except in relation to the social crises and dislocations of post-war Europe and America. At no time in the history of Christian thought has theological reconstruction been so thoroughgoing as in our generation—a result of the findings of science, the development of technology, and the new social experiments.

It is this insight that makes it possible for the modern mind, in a way impossible before, to distinguish between the function of religion as the integration and revaluation of the values involved in all the practical interests and activities of the common life and the instruments by which the function of religion finds expression—theology, ritual, and the ecclesiastical institution. The function remains constant; but the structures of theological belief, ceremonial, and institution undergo constant change as the practical interests and activities of the group from which they are derived change. It is of the greatest importance that this distinction between function and structure be made. Sectarianism arises when the variant reli-

4 *The Atonement and the Social Process* (New York: Macmillan Co., 1930).

gious groups within society fail to make this distinction and are betrayed into identifying their particular theological formulations, their ceremonials, and their ecclesiastical polities with religion as a function of human experience. Religion at the functional level is unitive; at the theological, sacramental, and ecclesiastical level it becomes divisive and sectarian.

As long as religion is vital and creative, it is not set off from the rest of personal and social experience, thus taking its place alongside other specialized and particular interests. It operates at the integrating center of all types of experience. It is when religion migrates from the integrating center of a people's life to the periphery and becomes preoccupied with its theological formulas, rituals, and institutional structures that it loses its essentially religious character in the qualitative sense and becomes religion in the substantive sense.[5]   It loses its sensitivity to social issues and its capacity for radical social criticism and reconstruction. It then becomes just another narrowly specialized interest pursued as an end in itself, comparable with detached economics, politics, and intellectual activities. It becomes formal, backward-looking, authoritative. This type of religion has shown a tendency to set itself against discoveries of science and new forms of social living, thus acting as a drag upon social progress. In the end, after futile resistance, it belatedly accepts the new insights that have arisen from the common life, often outside organized religion, and incorporates them into its own thought and life. Thus detached religion itself becomes secular and, while righteously protesting against secularism, through its further fragmentation of culture becomes a major contributor to the secularizing process.

Considerations such as these raise the fundamental question as to whether a sectarian church is capable of providing an

[5] Professor Dewey was the first to make this distinction, in *A Common Faith* (New Haven, Conn.: Yale University Press, 1934).

adequate program of religious education for the whole community. The facts of the period when sectarian religion was excluded from the public schools abundantly justified the action. Subsequent sectarian attitudes fully justify the conclusion that the inclusion of sectarian religion at the present time would be no less disastrous. These considerations raise the further question as to whether the community as such must not assume the responsibility for the teaching of religion on a functional and nonsectarian basis.

III

This analysis of the functional nature of education and religion brings us directly to a re-examination of the relation of church and state in a democracy. (An examination of the history of the doctrine of the separation of church and state makes it evident that the principle rests upon a structural rather than upon a functional relation of these two institutions. Since the disestablishment of the Congregational church in New England and of the Anglican church in Virginia, church and state have been institutionally separate in America.) The American idea of a free church in a free society has been one of the most constructive contributions to a problem that has through centuries vexed European nations. Of the validity of this principle there is little doubt among Americans—even among the Catholics, who, while not admitting its validity as a universal principle, are convinced that it is best in the United States. Nor is there any likelihood that the electorate will ever, in the light of American experience, consent to the abandonment of this principle.

(Nevertheless, while institutionally separate, they have never been functionally so. Members of the church are also, at the same time, members of the state, and vice versa. The titles of churches to property are guaranteed by the state. The exemption of church property from taxation is in reality a subsidy by the state. In many commonwealths the clergy derive their right to perform weddings from license by the state. The Constitution and the Bill of Rights specifically guarantee to the churches freedom to worship God according to their own consciences. The coinage of the nation bears the inscription, "In God We Trust." High public officials take their oath of office on the Bible. Every session of Congress is opened with prayer for God's guidance. Credits from church-supported schools are validated by the state. Washington on his knees at Valley Forge and Lincoln seeking divine guidance and support during the Civil War are symbols of the way in which the heads of state have turned to God in times of national crisis. On the other hand, the attitudes of church constituencies, sometimes expressed through lobbies and pressure blocs, have profoundly influenced legislation, as in the Prohibition Amendment, the anti-evolution law in Tennessee, and the defeat of the child-labor amendment. The defeat of Alfred E. Smith, a Catholic, for the presidency is a case in point. Many members of the state and national legislative, judicial, and executive branches of government are churchmen whose opinions and acts are greatly influenced by the churches of which they are members.

Such considerations as these lead us directly to the conclusion that the relationship of church and state is grounded in the fundamental fact of the community as the ultimate social reality in national life. All that has been said about religion sustaining a functional relation to the total community is equally to be said about government's being a function of the whole community. Government is the community regulating itself by laws, levying taxes upon itself to carry the burden of public expenditure, maintaining economic and diplomatic relations with other nations, raising armies and navies to protect itself against aggressors, maintaining courts to adjudicate the rights of citizens, creating and regulating currency, maintaining a police force to guarantee the peace, and supporting and supervising education. Under the simpler frontier conditions in America these functions were, on the whole, negatively conceived as the guaranties of inalienable rights. Under the more complex conditions of contemporary American life these functions are coming to be positively conceived, as evidenced by social planning, the extension of social services, and the equalizing of opportunity between the privileged and the underprivileged groups in the population. As in the case of religion, a distinction is to be made between government and the state. The state is the institutional structure for the performance of the governmental functions of the community. For the same reason, political theory, party politics, and the state are never to be identified with government any more than theology, ceremonial, or the church are to be identified with religion. As Professor Robert L. Calhoun has pointed out, both the church and the state are social institutions that arise out of the ultimate fact of community and that serve different functions in that community.[6]

The relations of church and state, therefore, take place on two levels. On the structural, or institutional, level they are frequently in competition, if not in conflict. In the long and troubled struggle between them each has shown totalitarian tendencies to attempt to control the other and the whole life of the community, as in the struggle of the emperors and popes in Europe from the ninth to the fourteenth centuries, in the Third Reich and in Japan at the present time, and in the refusal of the British Parliament to permit the Anglican church to revise its prayer book. On the functional level, on the other hand, each, in its fulfilment of its functions in the community, complements and mutually supports the other. On this level they have never been separate or in competition, and, in the nature of the social process, they never can be. As creatures of

[6] H. P. Van Dusen, R. L. Calhoun, *et al.*, *Church and State in the Modern World* (New York: Harper & Bros., 1937).

the comprehending community, both serve the needs of the community and are answerable to it. As mutually supporting phases of the whole community, each owes to the other constructive criticism which, however, should never approach the use of coercion.

The solution of the problem of the relation of religion to education must, therefore, be sought on the functional level where religion and government as mutually supporting functions of the comprehending American community interact in meeting the needs of the community. These needs of the whole people are interrelated needs that cannot be separated from the living tissue of interaction that is the American community. These needs are not only for food, shelter, legal justice, and physical security but also for a fundamental orientation toward reality, for spiritual values and convictions that lend meaning and dignity to the life of the common man, and for commitment to those transcendent ends that unite a people in their imaginations and emotions in the fulfilment of a destiny in keeping with the fatherhood of God and the brotherhood of man. Man's religious needs are not dissociated from his other needs. They are all his needs—intellectual, economic, political, aesthetic, and moral—set in the context of man's widest relations to the whole of reality and lifted to a conscious level of responsibility to God as the ground of that reality.

It will be seen that it is at the point of their functional relation to the community that education, religion, and the relation of church and state find their common rootage in the common life. It is here that they find, not only their essential characters, but their mutually supporting relation to one another. It is here that the solution of the problem of the relation of religion to education in democratic American society must be sought.

IV

TOWARD A CONSTRUCTIVE SOLUTION
THE SCHOOL

To seek the solution of our problem in the structural relations of church and state, as in the past, not only is to locate it in the area of conflict but is to distort it and to falsify the essential nature of education, religion, and government. The earlier solution of the problem on this basis, as we have seen, was only palliative and has created for our generation a much more complex and difficult one. A functional approach seems to render the problem much more manageable by pointing in the direction of a division of responsibility among mutually supporting agencies.

On the basis of the foregoing survey of the historical evolution of the educational situation in America and of an analysis of the fundamental assumptions concerning the functional nature of education, the functional relation of religion to experience, and the functional relation of church and state, we are now in a position to inquire as to the implications of these considerations for a constructive solution of the problem of religion in education. It appears obvious that in approaching a solution of the problem under present conditions a quite different orientation toward it is required from that with which it was approached when the earlier solution was adopted. It would also appear that any fruitful proposal must rest upon a well-considered philosophy regarding the nature of education, the nature of religion, and the relation of church and state. In the absence of such a philosophy piecemeal experiments are likely to be atomistic and fruitless and may do more harm than good. Ill-considered experiments may even issue in arousing the old antagonisms, with the result that the problem may be rendered more difficult, if not insoluble, for a long time to come.

Manifestly, we are yet in the early discussional stages of the consideration of this problem. Growing out of the meeting of minds at this exploratory stage there should be a clarification of the issues involved and a number of proposals that will lend themselves to criticism and experimentation in different types of situations in the hope that a national pattern may in time emerge. What is here proposed, therefore, is in the nature of a suggestion that seems to the writer to be indicated by a review of the historical facts and an analysis of the fundamental assumptions involved. If it appears to be tentative and confined to the larger outlines of a procedure, this is due to the fact that it falls within the period of exploration of possibilities that in the nature of the case yet await the confirmation of experimentation.

I

A review of the various attempts on the part of the churches to provide religious education for all the children and young people of the nation, as set forth in chapter ii, seems to warrant the conclusion that none of them offers a satisfactory solution of the problem of the relation of religion to education. Not only are they failing to reach more than half of the children and youth of the nation, but, under the limitations which circumstances impose upon them, they are, as education, far from satisfactory. Even if they could qualify on both these points, the fundamental division of the education of the whole self into the secular and the religious could not be justified on the grounds of either a sound educational philosophy or a modern functional concept of the relation of religion to personal and social experience. The most promising of these procedures—that of the weekday church school as carried on in its several forms by the three major religious faiths—still leaves the major issues unsolved by separating religion from the rest of education; by perpetuating, even in mitigated form, the sectarianism of religion; and by failing to reach the entire school population.

Neither can there be any justification, even under the pressures of the present situation, in reintroducing sectarian religious teaching into the public schools. Subsequent experience indubitably proves that the original solution was right in excluding sectarian religion from public education. Its fault lay in the fact that it did not go far enough in discovering ways by which religion could be retained as an integral part of education without its sectarian elements. With such concepts of the nature of religion as then generally prevailed it was impossible that such ways could have been foreseen. Their discovery had to wait upon the relatively recent insights into a functional, rather than a theological or ecclesiastical, understanding of religion made possible by its scientific study. Such insights now make it possible to advance upon the constructive contribution of the older solution to a more inclusive and satisfactory resolution of the problem.

In the meantime, on one point the American people appear to have reached a clear-cut and unalterable conviction—that education for all the people in a democracy is a function of the state. Under our constitutional right of religious liberty they are perfectly willing to grant to any religious body the right and privilege of offering sectarian education in its own schools if its conviction leads it to do so. But by legislation and court decisions the people seem irrevocably committed to the policy that public funds shall not be diverted to the use of sectarian schools, or that public schools shall not, as was the case in some instances with Catholic public schools, include sectarian schools as a part of their system.

What is here proposed, therefore, is that nonsectarian religion as a phase of culture should be included as an integral part of public education. This proposal is based upon a functional concept of the nature and ends of education, a functional concept of the relation of religion to personal and social experience, and a functional concept of the relation of church and state as different aspects of the community as the ultimate social reality. It is based also upon the conviction that in American society the public school is the most authentic interpreter of the American way of life, that education is a responsibility of all the people functioning through the instrumentalities of the state, and that the separation of church and state as institutions should be inviolably maintained in American democracy.

II

Specifically, there are six ways in which religion conceived functionally and as a phase of culture may be included in the program of the public school on a nonsectarian basis, in complete conformity with the above principles and as the apparent logical outcome of their implications. These suggested methods of approach are to be construed not as alternatives but as six different concomitant aspects of an inclusive procedure.

1. Religion should be objectively dealt with wherever it is encountered in the subject matter of the regular curriculum. In doing this the school need not, and should not, go out of its way to bring religion in. Neither should it be dealt with in a moralistic or hortatory manner. It should receive the same realistic treatment as any other aspect of culture.

Enough has been said in chapter ii in connection with the cultural heritage of children and young people to indicate the component place of religion in the great traditions of culture —in literature, in history, in philosophy, in the social sciences, and in the arts. Religion cannot be neglected in the consideration of these fields of knowledge without distorting and mutilating them. As was there pointed out, it is impossible to con-

[60]

vey any adequate understanding or appreciation of the great masterpieces of literary expression without giving due attention to the Bible and the volume of religious classics through the centuries. Whether history is conceived as a narrative of events or as the science of the progressive development of human society in the light of the operation of social, physical, economic, or intellectual factors, no account of human progress can be adequate that omits religious events or the influence of man's concern with religious values upon the shaping of his career. It is inconceivable that education should attempt to introduce the young to philosophy as man's attempt to discover meanings in the events of his experience and to organize them into consistent systems of thought without including his religious speculations upon his relation to reality as it affects his destiny. As a form of collective behavior religion constitutes an important part of man's associated life with which the social sciences are concerned. In the field of art, its whole tradition is mutilated and deprived of one of its primary motifs if religious expressions in architecture, painting, sculpture, and music are ignored.

While it may be granted that the public schools have always incidentally taught a great deal about religion through reference in history courses to the church during the medieval and early Christian periods and through study of the great religious classics in courses in literature, it cannot be maintained that such treatment constitutes a conscious and intentional attempt to show in a systematic way the functional relation of religion to these several aspects of an evolving culture such as is exhibited in the teaching of literature, history, philosophy, the social sciences, or the arts as major concerns of the curriculum.

So much we have already pointed out with respect to the older traditions that constitute so large a part of the school curriculum. But a more extended comment than has thus far been made concerning the religious possibilities of science may be offered. Formerly it was thought that science and religion, at least as traditionally conceived, were in conflict with each other. It now begins to appear that no phase of modern man's culture has greater implications for religion, functionally conceived, than science. The sciences—each in its separate field—have, in their discovery of uniformities of natural phenomena and causal relations between events, laid the sure foundations of a concept of a universe with which man may, through intelligence, enter into effective relationship. Once quite isolated in their search for sequences and relationships in particular fields, the sciences have in more recent years become aware of the interrelatedness of phenomena, as in biochemistry and social psychology. There is now emerging a unitive science which rests upon this interrelatedness of phenomena, whether physical, chemical, biological, psychological, or social. A new emphasis is being placed upon continuity throughout the phenomenal world. This new movement is characterized by an increasing tendency on the part of scientists to stress the operational effects of their findings in human society rather than abstract scientific formulas. This emphasis is carrying science beyond the once accepted self-imposed limits of detached disinterestedness to a growing sense of social responsibility. It is bringing scientific thought into the realm of values as well as that of techniques. In view of the social consequences of the products of science, this movement is emphasizing a scale of values in relation to human and social ends which carries the discrimination of values to the level of the revaluation of values. The extent and the significance of this movement are evidenced by the work of the Congress for the Unification of Science; the *International Encyclopedia of Unified Science;* the Conference on Science, Philosophy, and Religion; the recent round-table discussions of the American Association for the Advancement of Science; and the creation of an interdivisional committee on unified science at the University of

Chicago, which, as far as the writer knows, is the first attempt on the part of a university to integrate its scientific research and teaching.

This movement toward the integration of a world view based upon unitive science has profound religious significance. As Edward F. Haskell has recently pointed out:

> Unified science is, like all religions, inescapably and directly connected with values, ethics, and morals. And values are connected with action. The religious force of unified science (unlike that of most other world-views) is manifested in integrated knowledge, mutually comprehensible speech, and uncompromisingly social action. . . . . In short, unified science gives the power of knowledge, of faith, and of efficient action to the individual and to society. This power is the religious force of unified science.[1]

Perhaps it is not going beyond the evidence to suggest that science so conceived is more effective in the evocation of religious attitudes and religious commitment to the realities of life than are the traditional theological formulations and symbols that arose for the most part out of a prescientific culture and that now, having lost their articulation with the real and present world of man's experience, have become secular and divisive.

Even so brief a sketch of the possibilities of the several fields of knowledge dealt with in the subject matter of public education would seem to make obvious the resources of these fields for religious use and at the same time to point out the impossibility of dealing with them objectively and realistically if their religious content and implications are neglected.

2. Religion may well be included in public education as a field of knowledge comparable with the fields of literature, natural science, history, philosophy, the social sciences, and the arts. As was pointed out in chapter iii, religious behavior is as amenable to observation, description, analysis, and appraisal as any other form of human behavior. It has as rich a

[1] "The Religious Force of Unified Science," *Scientific Monthly*, June, 1942.

subject matter as any other field of knowledge dealt with in the school curriculum. On every ground, therefore, there is as much reason for making religion a field of special study as there is for making science, literature, history, philosophy, and the arts fields of special study.

Religion has a voluminous literature. The history of religion is as complex as the history of any other phase of culture, and it is coextensive with man's career on this planet. It is rich in speculative thought as expressed in its theological systems and in its philosophy of religion. It has built for itself throughout the ages institutional structures comparable with those of the family and the state. It has developed a language of signs, symbols, and gestures comparable with the technical language of science, philosophy, or the arts.

There is every argument for religion's being included as a special subject at the level of general education, since, on grounds already advanced, it is impossible to understand or appreciate historical culture or contemporary life without taking religion into account. On the same grounds there is every reason why the student at the higher levels of advanced study should be given the opportunity to specialize in the field of religion, just as he is now given opportunity to specialize in other fields of interest, and to use the same methods of critical analysis and research that are employed in other fields.

It may not be amiss to point out that establishing a special field of religion does not relieve the other fields of knowledge of the responsibility of dealing adequately with religion wherever it occurs in the other subjects of the curriculum. In establishing a special field, religion encounters the same danger that all other departmentalized subjects encounter. It is the danger of compartmentalization. Whereas man's interaction with the various aspects of his world is a unitive process, the division of education into specialized fields has too often resulted in the pursuit of certain disciplines as ends in themselves, without perception of their interrelatedness with other fields of knowledge.

To whatever extent danger is incurred in the departmentalization of other fields of knowledge, it is especially present in the case of religion. This arises from the fact of the comprehensive character of religion, which involves all other interests and activities. As has been pointed out, at the level of experience it is a quality that is diffused throughout the whole range of personal and social living. In primitive societies no one would think of religion as a separate and special interest because it is so much a phase of the whole of life. In the most creative periods of religion neither the leaders nor the people would have thought of using the word "religion." The eighth-century prophets did not, but they considered every aspect of the common life, whether economic or political, from a religious point of view. Jesus never used the word "religion" but faced life in terms of the actual situations which it presented in the light of religious values. In a vitally religious society religion is primarily a qualitative matter and only secondarily a substantive matter—a specialized field of interest in itself.

3. The school can give the growing person an actual experience of the higher spiritual values involved in the relationships of the school community. There is abundant evidence to support the conclusion that of all the influences that abide in the experience of students, the greatest is that of participation in the school community. Second in rank comes the influence of teachers and last of all the formal courses of study. This is especially true of the elementary and secondary levels of education, less true of students who have entered upon specialization at the advanced levels of higher education and research. It is in the manifold relations of the school community—person-to-person, person-to-group, and group-to-group—that many of the most productive educational experiences arise. These relations involve adjustments, values, appreciations, and

commitments. And, precisely because participation in the school community involves these elements, it is particularly potentially productive of religious attitudes and motives. As Professor John Macmurray has pointed out, the structure of religious experience is determined by the many-sided relationships in which the living person is involved.[2]

To this end, Dr. Ernest J. Chave recently spent several months visiting elementary classrooms, observing and recording the situations arising in the normal course of school experiences in which essentially religious values are involved. Out of these records he has deduced ten categories that are basically religious. These are: a sense of the worth of persons, development of social sensitivity, growth in appreciation of the universe, growth in the discrimination of values, growth in the sense of responsibility and accountability, recognition of the need for co-operative fellowship, recognition that the quest for truth and the realization of ideals is a slow and endless pursuit, development of a working philosophy of life, observance of special times and ceremonies, and development of adequate means of expression of spiritual values and goals.

It is not enough that the situations involving these religious values be casually encountered and passed over. The growing persons need to be made aware of the values involved and to experience them as vivid and convincing realities. These situations need to be lifted into consciousness, to be reflected upon, and to have their potential values made explicit. Moreover, as experienced values, having their origin in the concrete relations of the school community, they need to find expression in the fuller perception and fulfilment of these relations. In this light it is clear that the experiences of the school community present one of the richest sources of religious insight, attitudes, and motives. But to be productive they must be experienced,

[2] *The Structure of Religious Experience* (New Haven, Conn.: Yale University Press, 1936).

not merely talked about. It is doubtful if anything is to be gained by attempting to channel them into traditional theological formulas. It may not even be necessary to label them as religious. Such discussion of them as may be necessary for their clarification and implications should always be with reference to the completed act as the fulfilment of relations.

4. The school can do much in the cultivation of religious attitudes by the use of ceremonials and celebrations. Many of these are deeply imbedded in American custom and have long ceased to be the exclusive property of any religious sect. Such are the great seasonal celebrations like Thanksgiving, Christmas, New Year's, and Easter. Others are concerned with the great moving events of American history and with its outstanding leaders. Many appropriate celebrations might well arise out of the significant experiences of the school community itself. The ultimate origin of all celebrations is the meaningful experience of the common life. Every school community, out of the richness and meaningfulness of its own experience, might well, through symbolic and dramatic celebration, create symbols and occasions that would serve to lift out and idealize the events and values that have had meaning for it. By the confession of most educators, not enough opportunity is offered in the routine of school procedure for the stimulation and noble expression of the emotions. A little imagination and creativity on the part of teachers and young people will find ready at hand abundant materials for the expression of group values through the noble forms of art.

Furthermore, there is in the use of the classical symbols and celebrations of the great religious faiths an opportunity for creating understanding and appreciation of the beliefs and practices of the great religious faiths, Protestant, Catholic, and Jewish. Such understanding and appreciation go far beyond mere toleration. The University of Michigan has found it very fruitful, both culturally and religiously, to bring together on the occasion of its "parleys" what it designates as "the great religious traditions" represented on the campus. Beyond the universal elements of religious faith and symbols, each of these great "traditions" possesses a uniquely rich content of thought and feeling that, when interpreted sympathetically, leads to appreciation and mutual respect. It is a mistake to seek tolerance and co-operation through attempting to reduce the various types of religious experience to their minimal common elements of agreement. This leads to meaningless abstraction. Richness of appreciation is more likely to come through sincere attempts to understand the full-bodied content of thought and feeling that often arises in differences. The school, as the one common meeting place of all the component elements in the community, offers an unusually favorable opportunity for such a common sharing of the attitudes and ideals of the various groups that constitute its common life. The use of folk costumes, folk dances, folk music, and folk arts and crafts in developing understanding and appreciation of national groups might well serve as a pattern in developing understanding and appreciation of religious differences.

5. Public education will do well to explore the possibilities of religion as a principle of the integration of education and the culture which education seeks to interpret. One of the distinguishing characteristics of secularism is the tendency of culture to fall apart into more or less unrelated fragments, with the consequent loss of its meaning and sense of worth. This has for some time been the tendency in Western and American culture. It may be said to constitute one of the most urgent and difficult problems of contemporary civilization. Inevitably, this fragmentation of culture has found expression in education. The division of education into specialized fields has resulted in the cultivation of the several fields of knowledge as ends in themselves, without adequate recognition of their interrelatedness with other fields of knowledge. The result is not

only atomism in education but an increasing dissociation of education from the life-process. The problem of synthesis in education is coming to the fore as one of the crucial issues of educational theory and practice. Numerous experiments are under way in attempting to overcome this defect of overspecialization, such as interest groupings of subjects, survey courses, comprehensive examinations, co-operative courses, and the focusing of the several fields of knowledge upon specific problems of contemporary life. Various principles of integration have been proposed, such as metaphysics by President Robert Maynard Hutchins,[3] a core of fundamental values by President H. D. Gideonse,[4] theology by Professor William Adams Brown,[5] and religion in the broader sense by Dr. Charles Clayton Morrison.[6]

Historically, there have been four great factors that have contributed to the integration of a people's culture—philosophy in terms of systems of thought, art in terms of appreciation, religion in terms of practical values, and great causes, such as the Crusades or the present war. As has been previously suggested, there is promise of a new principle of synthesis in unitive science. Among these influences both history and psychology would particularly stress the integrative effectiveness of religion. The great historic periods of cultural unity have been periods of religious faith. Religion, functionally understood, is by its essential nature a comprehending and integrating experience. It is not something set apart from the rest of life but a quality that diffuses itself throughout every area of experience. Its concepts and practices are rooted in the prac-

[3] *The Higher Learning in America* (New Haven, Conn.: Yale University Press, 1936).

[4] *The Higher Learning in a Democracy* (New York: Farrar & Rinehart, 1937).

[5] *The Case for Theology in the University* (Chicago: University of Chicago Press, 1938).

[6] "President Hutchins' Mistake" (editorial), *Christian Century*, April 4, 1937.

[69]

tical interests and activities of the common life. One of the two functions of religion is to revalue these interests and activities and to unite them into a total meaning and worth of life in terms of its responsible relation to God. Its other function is to subject every practical interest and activity of the common life to cross-criticism and reconstruction in the light of this core of fundamental values. Thus religion is not merely contemplative or appreciative, as in the case of philosophy and art, but is concerned with practical, operative values which find their fulfilment in action.

It would seem, therefore, that religion offers unique resources for bringing order and unity into the present chaos of education when it is properly related to the other great means by which man has achieved integration in his culture.

6. The school, as is increasingly being done, can use the resources of religion in its rapidly expanding program of personal counseling. Education is more and more concerned with the adjustment of the whole self to its physical and social environment. In its more progressive modes education is no longer concerned merely with courses of study or with the transmission of knowledge or the development of skills. It is concerned also with the resolution of emotional conflicts that lead to the frustration and disintegration of personality. Even more, it is concerned with the wholesome development of personality through such an organization of emotions that these self-destroying conflicts will not arise. Because of its antagonism to certain regimenting theological concepts that create emotional conflict, psychiatry has in the past avoided religion as a potential resource for mental therapy. But of late it is becoming evident to many psychiatrists that the resolution of emotional conflicts involves the organization of ideals, a scale of values, faith in an ordered universe, and a working world view. The testimony of Dr. Jung, above cited, confirms this tendency.

A study of the experiences of high-school students, made under the direction of the writer, reveals the fact that these tensions exist to a far greater extent than most parents and teachers realize. Many of the conflicts are created, not only by adjustments required in the school community, but by teachers and parents themselves. This study also reveals that in many schools, if the population studied is fairly representative, little awareness of this need of children and young people exists and little is being done to meet it. One of the most promising new developments in an increasing number of progressive schools is the attention that is being given to personal counseling as a fundamental part of the education of childhood and youth.

III

The practical difficulties of including functional religion in the program of the public schools are confessedly very great. One is that teachers who may still be under the influence of stereotypes of sectarian religious thinking will identify the theology and polity of their particular sects with religion. Another is the problem of method, which in the older fields of the social studies has in the better schools achieved a degree of objectivity, inquiry, and freedom of discussion. Another is the pressure of powerful religious groups in the community that, like other pressure groups, might seek to dominate the schools. Still another is the presence of minority groups, including those who are avowedly nonreligious, who may not wish their children to be taught religion or who cannot see beyond the limits of their particular religious views to the universal elements of functional religion. However, the schools have throughout their history encountered problems of similar magnitude and difficulty and are by no means free from them in other fields. Such difficulties, however great, constitute no reason for the schools' not advancing in the light of the best thought of our generation and in the interest of the needs of children and youth and of public welfare. Rather, they are to be faced, understood, and resolved by patient and democratic procedures.

Obviously, if nonsectarian religion is to become an integral part of public education, it will be necessary to include religion in the professional training of teachers. Such specialized training is now required of teachers of science, history, literature, and the arts. Manifestly, no less careful training is to be expected of teachers of religion, especially in view of the fact that (at least, so it seems to us with our sectarian backgrounds) religion is the most difficult of all fields to teach. It cannot be left to undisciplined teachers who have not learned to distinguish between a particular theology or ecclesiastical polity and the nonsectarian function of religion. Such untrained teachers are likely to interpret religion in terms of their own particular sect and their own personal sectarian loyalties.

Furthermore, if religion is to be dealt with as it appears in the several fields of knowledge, it may be necessary to include religion as a fundamental part of the training of all teachers. At the moment, such a procedure is being contemplated in certain state teachers colleges.[7]

At this point the question of method inevitably arises. Is it possible to deal objectively in the school with a subject so emotionally charged in a community in which so many sectarian differences exist? Will the dominant religious groups in the community reach into the school and by indirect, if not by direct, pressures control the teachers and the teaching of religion to the disadvantage of minority groups?

This is by no means a problem peculiar to the teaching of religion. It is a problem faced by every progressive school which seeks to deal with the living issues of personal and social living. The traditional school is not troubled by this problem. It is content to confine itself to tradition and what is written in textbooks, thus avoiding all controversial subjects. But a crea-

[7] E.g., the Northwest Teachers College of Missouri.

tive education that is concerned with living issues in community life and with social reconstruction finds itself in many areas of conflict. This is particularly true of the field of economics and political theory, where differences of opinion and highly emotionalized prejudice are involved—perhaps even more violent differences and emotions than in the field of religion. But the school does not draw back on that account. It has been developing a new pattern of learning—that of inquiry, comparison of diverse points of view, suspended judgment, weighing of evidence, and making up one's mind in the light of facts. This is precisely what the citizen in a democracy is called upon to do in making decisions in regard to public policy and by his vote in responsibly participating in the determination of such policy. Education in a democracy, we are coming to see, not only must introduce the growing citizen to the issues of social living but must develop in him, through actual experience in making decisions, the attitudes, methods of thought, and skills necessary for assuming active responsibility in a society in which government is of the people, by the people, and for the people.

Religion as an objective form of social behavior is, like the atom, a chemical compound, or a social institution something to be understood in its nature and function and not something to be defended or made the subject of propagandist support. The appropriate methods for such treatment of religion in public education as is here proposed are the same as those employed in the treatment of all other subjects in the curriculum. Fortunately, the results of historical research make the use of such methods possible in the study of the Bible, the history of religion, the evolution of religious ideas, the development of religious institutions, and the philosophy of religion.

It is to be hoped that such a treatment of religion would result, not in a mere knowledge of facts about religion, but in an experience of the processes of religion as it operates in the common life and in an experience of religious values. Progressive education, by introducing the young to an experience of life, is seeking to avoid the danger of teaching the great traditions as end-products of past human experience. Too often in the traditional school has language been "taught" in terms of its structure apart from the actual experience of communication, record, and the clarification of thought. So also mathematics has been taught as a formal discipline apart from the experience of the quantitative aspects of human living. History, likewise, has too often been taught as dates and events without the learner's being given an experience of process, of becoming, of which history is the interpretative record. Many students have had courses in science without the experience of science as a method of thought or as a means of redirecting personal and social experience. Likewise, the mere teaching of facts about religion would be comparably sterile unless the student were to experience the movement and growth of values that lie back of all the historical and contemporary expressions of religion.

In connection with method another problem arises—that of members of the community, usually minority groups, who do not want their children and young people to be exposed to the teaching of religion. This problem is grounded in the sectarian and propagandist phases of religion. Propaganda and sectarianism go together. In the public school there is no place for either. The task of public education is to provide opportunity for the understanding of religion just as it is to provide opportunity for the understanding of all other aspects of the culture in which all are participants. Whether one likes it or not, religion has been and is a part of that culture—a culture that cannot be understood or appreciated when the fact of religion is omitted or obscured. When such objections are analyzed, it frequently turns out that the objection of the so-called "irreligious" minorities is not at all to religion as a phase of culture but rather to the identification of religion with sectarian theological formulas or sectarian ecclesiasticism. Some of the most religious persons the writer has known are those who have preferred not to be identified with any particular theological system or sect but who in their deepest attitudes and motives are profoundly religious. This was true of Abraham Lincoln. The fact that one may or may not agree with a particular economic or political theory is no reason why it should not be understood through the objective and impartial processes of democratic education. In a democracy acceptance or rejection of any point of view on the basis of enlightened conviction is a fundamental principle of education.

In view of these difficulties it would seem the part of wisdom that small-scale experiments should be undertaken under wise and careful supervision in selected communities where there is a relative homogeneity of population and where the initial difficulties are not too great. Above all, such experiments should be undertaken in communities where there is a sense of need and where the constituent elements of the population are of a mind to undertake an adventure in understanding and cooperation. A wholesale introduction of religion on a functional basis into the program of general education, especially where there is unwillingness to have it introduced and where the attitudes of tolerance and co-operation are lacking, would almost certainly evoke negative reactions that would jeopardize the entire effort at the solution of a problem that is extremely sensitive and difficult. In the solution of a problem so complex and difficult time and patience will be required so that a theoretical approach may be constantly checked and corrected by experience.

IV

It has often been said by sectarian zealots that the school is a godless institution. Nothing could be further from the truth. This charge was frequently and vehemently made during the period in which Horace Mann was fighting the battle in Massachusetts to free the schools from sectarian control—it was made in spite of the fact that Mann himself, a genuinely religious person, openly expressed the view that religion was a necessary support for character as the chief end of education and advocated the reading of the Bible without comment in the schools. An equally bitter and unjust charge of atheism was launched by certain clergy against Thomas Jefferson in connection with his efforts to disestablish the church in Virginia, though Jefferson was deeply religious, proposed plans by which religion could be taught in connection with the University of Virginia, and himself translated the New Testament. No doubt, in the early antagonism between educational authorities and sectarian zealots, resulting from the exclusion of sectarian religion from the schools, some ground was provided for this charge by the criticism of sectarian bigotry on the part of some "emancipated" teachers who saw in the sectarian manifestation of religion only superstition or obscurantism. These critics were victims of the same error as that of the sectarian zealots whom they criticized—identifying dogmatic theology and ecclesiasticism with religion—besides being as dogmatic as the dogmatists whom they criticized. In more recent years, however, with the lessening of the old tensions, this criticism by minority groups in both the school and the church has practically ceased. Instead, there has been a growing respect on the part of educators for religion and a growing appreciation on the part of the churches for what the schools are doing.

The teachers in the American schools are among the most idealistic members of society. Many of them are devotedly religious and active in the various forms of organized religion. Many of them are motivated and sustained in their work by high religious incentives. The influence of their religious attitudes upon their students is profound. As a matter of fact, in these personal attitudes of teachers and in their reverence in handling the subject matters they teach, religion is and always has been in the public schools. Despite the fact that the schools do not formally teach religion, they are anything but godless. Not a few observers are even convinced that religion is a more vital experience in some state universities than in some church-related colleges.

Religion is no more a prerogative of the churches than education is a prerogative of the schools. Both are, in the last analysis, functions of the community. To the extent that churches and schools lose their articulation with the going life of the community they cease to be religious, on the one hand, or educational, on the other. Both the churches and the schools are under the judgment of the community. The defects which have been brought under review by the present proposal are chargeable to a sectarian religion, on the one hand, and to an inadequate and ineffective education, on the other. A constructive solution of the problem proposes the reorientation of both religion and education toward a common responsibility that is grounded in the needs of children and young people and in the needs of the community.

V

TOWARD A CONSTRUCTIVE SOLUTION
THE CHURCH

FROM the foregoing discussion it seems clear that there are certain things in the teaching of religion for which the public school is better equipped than any other institution. It is equally evident that there are well-defined limitations to what the school as a public institution can undertake in the field of religious nurture. In an equitable division of responsibilities in the community there are important functions which the church by its nature is better equipped to perform than is any other institution. In the discharge of these respective functions the church and school are not set in opposition to each other, nor are they in competition. They mutually support and supplement each other. Such a relationship calls for mutual understanding and co-operation in the definition of objectives, the determination of content, and the use of procedures. Their relation to each other is determined by the needs of the community from which both derive their existence and which both serve.

As we have seen, the conditions under which the churches operate render them incapable of providing an adequate program of religious instruction for all the children and young people of the nation. This arises only in part from the sectarianism of religion in America. It arises also from the limited opportunities and equipment of the churches for such a large-scale educational responsibility. Moreover, the churches should not be expected to assume responsibility for teaching religion as a phase of culture. That responsibility properly belongs to the public school as the most authentic interpreter of the American way of life. Relieved of this responsibility, which properly does not belong to them, the churches would be free to discharge effectively those functions of religious nurture which they are best fitted to perform and which no other institution in the community can so well undertake.

I

The things which the several religious communions can do better than any other social institution arise only in part out of the sectarianism of religion in America. It is true that wide cleavages exist among the major religious faiths. The Jews, on the one hand, find it impossible to accept the distinctive beliefs of Christianity that split off from Judaism in the first century A.D. The Catholics, on the other hand, find it equally impossible to accept the distinctive beliefs of Protestantism that split off from Catholicism in the sixteenth century. Protestants, in turn, are divided into a multitude of sects ranging in belief from the various shades of fundamentalism to the various shades of liberalism. As long as these differences exist, especially among the major faiths, there seems to be little prospect in the immediate future of achieving a common ground necessary for concerted action in religious nurture among the major religious faiths.

Notwithstanding these differences, however, as was pointed out in chapter i, there has been in recent years a marked softening of these inherited differences which grew out of historical conditions in the past. There are many unmistakable signs of awareness of the universal elements in religion that transcend all differences of theological formulation and ecclesiastical polity.

These movements are evidences of a growing consciousness of the corporateness of the church as a social institution which in its inclusiveness transcends all differences of creed and polity among its constituent bodies. It is the church as an ecu-menical fellowship of men and women of differing formulations of belief, race, nationality, and culture committed to a common body of religious ideals and convictions, rather than the church in its sectarian aspects, that is capable of providing a religious nurture to the young that no other institution can offer. The spiritual functions out of which these services arise are the reason for the existence of a vital church in society. If, as a fellowship for the interpretation of religion and the cultivation of the religious life, the church did not exist, the community, in the nature of the social process, would create some such institution for the performance of these functions, just as it has created the school, the state, and the courts for the performance of their respective functions. It is to this fellowship of religious convictions and ideals, in its ecumenical and historical role as the concrete embodiment of religious attitudes in human life, rather than to the churches in their sectarian divisiveness that society looks for the expression of the religious way of life. It is the church universal, the communion of saints through many centuries of change, the symbol of religious faith, and the public expression of the religious way of life.

If, however, there still remain certain sects which feel that they are under obligation to indoctrinate their young in their particular theological formulations, they have the unequivocal right to do so under the provisions of the Constitution and the Bill of Rights and may do so without social criticism. This certainly is the concern of particular churches and not of public education or of the church universal. However, in the present state of the ecclesiastical mind, some communions may wish to assume this responsibility for some time to come.

II

There are certain functions which the church universal, as a religious fellowship set in a long tradition of thought and life, can perform that neither the public school nor any other social agency can perform.

1. It can make explicit, clarify, and bring to fulness of meaning the religious values involved in the experience of children and young people in the various areas of their relations with the natural, social, and cosmic world. For this the church has a language quite as appropriate to religion as the languages of the sciences and the arts are to their respective fields. This language consists of signs, symbols, and gestures. It is in part suitable for the expression of ideas; in part for the expression of the emotions.

If religious experience is to be intelligent, it must be subjected to critical and reflective thought that brings it into relation with the known facts regarding the nature of reality and the nature of man as disclosed by science and philosophy. Otherwise it is likely to be dominated by emotion or to remain amorphous or obscurantist. Religion as an organization of meanings and values has a solid and complex intellectual content, as the elaboration of the various theological systems shows. It is anomalous that for so long religion and science have been thought to be in conflict. If religion is to be a vital influence in the lives of young people, it must be amenable to the insights that have come to the searchers after truth in the laboratory and on the field of history as well as in the reflections of the theologian. Otherwise it is in danger of being relegated to the realms of superstition or outmoded tradition. It is the obligation of the church to assist its youth in facing and thinking through in constructive ways the problems which religious experience raises. The church can render no greater service to modern youth than to make the meanings of science, philosophy, and religious experience interchangeable in a consistent and rational universe of meanings and discourse.

This is the meaning of historical and contemporary theology. Theology is as necessary to the religious mind as theory is to the scientist or as metaphysical speculation is to the philosopher. It is, therefore, not a question of a theology or no theology, but of a theology that is consistent with the known facts of the modern world. Historical theology is a record of the reflection of the religious mind upon the data of religious experience. It has undergone reinterpretation and reformulation in the light of new discoveries and of changing operative social values. The history of Christian thought shows that its main struggles have been with issues raised by new contacts with philosophic thought, as in the case of Gnosticism in the first century, or with new scientific discoveries, as in the case of the Copernican theory in the sixteenth century, the theory of evolution in the nineteenth century, or the theory of relativity in the twentieth century. In each of these instances theology has been forced to re-examine its basic assumptions concerning the nature of God, of reality, and of man and to reformulate its positions. At no time in the history of Christian thought has this reconstruction been so thoroughgoing as in contemporary theology. The current reaction of neo-orthodoxy reveals how difficult these readjustments are. Here, in this area of the intellectual interpretation of religious experience in relation to the expanding intellectual and social life of man in the modern world, lies one of the greatest opportunities and responsibilities of the church. This is not a responsibility of the school. It is the function of a church sensitively aware of the fresh revelations of God in man's experience of a dynamic world.

2. The church, as no other institution can do, can set life in its universal context, where it can be viewed in the wide perspectives of relationships and of eternity. In these perspectives life can be intellectually understood and emotionally felt in its wholeness. Unquestionably, the tendency of modern life is toward atomism. Unless there is some such frame of reference, each experience tends to focus attention upon itself in

isolation, even in the simplest forms of society. Under modern conditions, however, life has become extremely complex. This is due in part to the findings of science, which have introduced us to the vastness and intricacy of the universe. It is due in part to the piling-up of massive bodies of knowledge, which requires specialization in narrow fields. It is due in part to the increasing differentiation of highly specialized and detached operations in industry. Social organization under the conditions of modern communication and transportation has passed from relatively small groups in which the individual was quite well adjusted to his environment to a planetary society which outruns our intellectual habits and our emotional attitudes. Science in its earlier stages has, through its almost exclusive use of the method of analysis, contributed to the fragmentation of life. To all these factors must be added the onrush of a rapidly changing experience which in volume and speed exceeds our capacity of assimilation. The result is confusion, on the one hand, and the tendency of life to fall apart, on the other. With the loss of the sense of the wholeness of life in relation to a rationally consistent and stable world, life loses its sense of reality and worth.

The church as a fellowship provides an environment in which, through its intellectual concepts and symbols, one's life is set in the framework of a consistent and orderly universe. The various experiences encountered through participation in the many-sided relations of living are set in the long and wide perspectives of eternity. Here it is possible for the individual to see and feel his life as a whole and to have a vivid sense of its reality and worth.

3. In the environment which the church provides, it is possible for the growing person to achieve a sense of at-homeness in the universe. Modern science has disclosed a universe that in its vastness and complexity is beyond the power of the imagination to grasp. Moreover, through its emphasis upon

uniform and invariable laws, it has built up a picture of the universe as a cold, impersonal, closed mechanism. The sheer vastness of the universe, together with its impersonal mechanisms, may well dwarf and overwhelm the finite human being and fill him with an unutterable sense of loneliness and helplessness. Neither does the human spirit find much more warmth and friendliness in a world of abstract philosophic thought, with its "absolutes," "essences," "forms," and "final causes." When to these intellectual factors is added the immense problem of the adjustment of the growing person to the various social groups, with the differing and often conflicting roles for which they call, one realizes the difficulty of finding one's place in the world and a sense of adequate adjustment and security.

Now, as every psychiatrist knows, a sense of isolation is one of the most disintegrating of all known factors in its influence upon personality. Something of its devastating effect is indicated by the fact that studies of suicide reveal that a sense of personal isolation is the chief cause of despair. The human spirit is capable of sustained resistance to pain, disaster, and defeat as long as it feels that it belongs to a significant and rational order of life and is a responsible participant in it.

The church presents an environment in which the primary emphasis is upon persons—persons in their relationships, not only to the immediate fellowship, but to the widest ranges of reality. The universe to which it introduces one is an order of existence in which values are supreme. And, because it is an order of values, it is a universe that is personal, since values do not exist apart from persons. Moreover, because the universe has produced persons, it is difficult to escape the conviction that, however much of a structure of law and order it may possess, it is also, and perhaps basically, personal. At the heart of the universe the church makes vividly real to its members the presence of God, who is not only creator and ruler of an ordered universe but a loving heavenly Father. In such a personal universe one feels not only that he belongs and has significance as a person but that he is a responsible participant in bringing its potential values to progressive fulfilment. Such a universe of concern and self-giving love is one's spiritual home where he finds understanding, sympathy, and security. From its warmth, spiritual kinship, and sustaining resources he derives an inner peace which a distraught world cannot give and which it cannot take away, and through it he achieves poise in the presence of conflict and crisis.

4. The church, as no other institution can do, provides a sustained and sustaining fellowship. Of the four basic "wishes" which Professor W. I. Thomas[1] believed to be innate in human nature and the satisfaction of which in reasonable measure is necessary to the wholesome development of personality —the wishes for new experience, recognition, intimacy, and security —the last three are realizable only through participation in a significant social group. Even the first, as it actually turns out in human experience, is for the most part achieved in human relations. Furthermore, as the social psychologist fully recognizes, one of the most determinative influences in the formation of human personality is the role which one assumes in a social group or which is assigned to him by the group. In view of the different and often conflicting roles which one is called upon to assume in many diverse groups, such as the home, the school, vocation, "social" organizations, and leisure-time associations, there is great need that somewhere there shall be a group from the viewpoint of which it will be possible to see these several roles in their relationships and to bring them under review and appraisal. Moreover, it is through participation in a like-minded fellowship of persons that the individual is able to face the issues of life and to meet its crises, up-

[1] W. I. Thomas and F. Znaniecki, *The Polish Peasant* (New York: Alfred A. Knopf, 1927).

borne by the association of a common life in which he shares his aspirations, successes, frustrations, and defeats with a sustained and sustaining group.

Now, it is as a fellowship that the church most nearly approaches its essential nature and function. From the communal life of the earliest Christians to the present, the church has emphasized what it has been pleased to call "the communion of saints." In its smallest and local units it consists of an immediate, intimate, and face-to-face association of like-minded persons who share a common body of ideals and convictions and who are committed to the realization of the Christian way of life in personal and social living. But the church is more than a local fellowship. As a brotherhood stemming from the fatherhood of God, it is an inclusive and universal fellowship. It is, in its essential character, ecumenical. It includes in its fellowship all men everywhere who share its common faith and its common loyalty to Christ and his cause. Thus it transcends all boundaries of nation, race, and culture. It is at the present moment of world conflict, as it has been throughout the centuries, the most universal of social institutions. The church has, however, more than geographical and cultural extension. It has a temporal extension as well. The church is set within a great historic tradition. It includes in its continuing fellowship all those who through the centuries have cherished and have sought to bring to realization the Christian way of life. This was the insight of the author of the Book of Hebrews, who sought to quicken the faith of second-generation Christians by reminding them that they were surrounded by a cloud of witnesses—the living dead. The present membership of the church represents only the latest of a long procession of generations who have been engaged in the age-long quest of the Christian hope and the Kingdom of God. Thus, to the sustaining resources of the immediate local fellowship that is the church are added the vast resources and spiritual prestige of a universal association that not only transcends all human differences of race and nation but spans the centuries with an unbroken tradition of aspiration, faith, and spiritual achievement.

5. In addition to affording a sustained and sustaining fellowship, the church provides a stimulating environment for the nurture of the religious life. Through its long experience in dealing with human need it has developed techniques for the enrichment and cultivation of religious experience. As a society of religious persons, it is specifically oriented toward religious values and toward God as the Creator and Sustainer of these values. Since religion involves above all an orientation of the whole self toward God as the ultimate ground of reality, the participation of the growing person in a society where such an orientation continuously prevails as a primary characteristic is of incalculable importance.

Within such an orientation a most important technique consists in releasing the growing person from the sense of guilt and assuring him of the constantly recurring possibility of making a new beginning. This is the meaning of the drama of redemption. Here, through penitence and the grace of God, there is forgiveness and a new birth. The self-destroying burden of guilt is removed, and the forgiven faces life as a new creature.

The new birth is not, however, limited to a single experience of change in attitude and motive and commitment. It is a process continuing throughout life. There is constant need of reorientation, of the rectification of one's attitudes and motives, and of new commitments. Therefore, in this fellowship there are provided means for self-examination, repentance, and rededication, through the confessional, prayer, worship, and the celebration of the eucharist. In theological terminology these are called the "means of grace," as indeed they are. They are the disciplines of the spiritual life, which comes to full fruition, not casually or automatically, but as the result of assiduous cultivation, nurture, and sustained purpose.

Not least of these techniques is corporate worship. Here, as a participant in a social act of devotion, the growing person stands face to face with the Living God, and his inmost thought and intention are exposed to view in the light of the eternal. Here, through ancient symbols freighted with meaning, his life in its fundamental relation to God is celebrated, and his commitments to that which is supremely real and worthful are renewed and deepened. The language of worship—symbols, music, hymns, gestures, prayers, rituals, and architecture—is the language of the emotions and is close to the language of art. Through social sharing these emotions are heightened and rendered more vivid. Worship provides the alternation of withdrawal from and participation in the complex onrush of immediate and conflicting experience necessary for seeing life in its relationships and for its constructive criticism. Here, in the presence of the eternal, events which in their poignant immediacy seem of major importance shrink to small proportions, while aspects of life that are lost sight of or that seem remote take on major proportions.

> Far off the noises of the world retreat;
> The loud vociferations of the street
> Become an indistinguishable roar,
> So, as I enter here from day to day,
> And leave my burden at the minster gate,
> Kneeling in prayer, and not ashamed to pray,
> The tumult of the time disconsolate
> To inarticulate murmurs dies away,
> While the eternal ages watch and wait.[2]

6. The church as a continuing fellowship presents the growing person with causes which call for loyalty and commitment, so necessary to the effective integration of the whole

[2] Henry W. Longfellow, in *Divina Commedia*.

self and for the wholesome release of personality. The church is more than a contemplative body. In its truest nature it has always thought of itself as having a redemptive mission in society. In so far as it is genuinely religious it not only seeks, as we have seen in chapter iii, to achieve an integration of all experience into a total meaning and worth of life in terms of its responsible relation to God, but it assumes a critical and reconstructive attitude toward society. It is committed by its nature to social action. The prophetic tradition is one of radical social criticism. The eighth-century prophets spoke, not in terms of abstract relations to God, but in terms of the concrete realities of the economic, social, and political conditions of the then-existing situation. From their point of view man's relation to God was not to be fulfilled by sacrifice or ceremonial but through active mercy and social justice.[3] The heart of the prayer which Jesus taught his disciples to pray was the socially expressed desire that God's Kingdom would come and his will be done on earth as it is in heaven.[4] At the heart of his teaching was the idea of the Kingdom of God, a social concept to be realized in the relations and processes of social living.

In line with the nature of religion and this prophetic tradition it is a primary function of the church as a religious fellowship to bring the searching criticism of spiritual values to bear upon every process, every institution, and every way of life operative in society. But its function is not merely that of criticism. Beyond criticism lies action at every point where members of the church, as members of the community or as citizens of the state, are involved in the processes of production and distribution, of making and administering laws, or of participating in community enterprises. In these ways the church bears the responsibility of serving as a creative and reconstructive force in the community, in the nation, and, under

[3] Mic. 6:8.
[4] Matt. 6:9–15.

modern conditions, in the world. Herein lie the specific causes to which commitment and devotion are required. Here lie the problems of economic justice, race relations, the rights of minority groups, war and peace, and, above all at this moment of the world's life, of building a new order of social relationships throughout the world that will insure an enduring peace based upon justice and good will.

Commitments within the church as a religious fellowship are more, however, than commitments to specific causes. For the Christian the supreme commitment is to a Person. As a historical figure, Jesus gathers up into himself as their supreme embodiment the ideals, the attitudes, and the motives that through the centuries have been cherished by the Christian community as the highest expression of the religious way of life. In him as a living Person these ideals, attitudes, and motives appear not as abstract virtues but as living flesh and blood. This, in its deepest and most dynamic sense, is the meaning of the Incarnation. Through this personal relation to Christ convictions and commitments are transmuted into a transcendent loyalty. The transforming influence of this personal loyalty to Jesus lies upon every page of the New Testament and subsequent Christian literature. The earliest disciples of Jesus thought of themselves as being committed not only to a way of life but above all else to Christ as his disciples. In their behavior they did not rationalize their decisions under the formula of subjecting each choice to a "cross-criticism of values" but rather made their decision in each practical situation under the conviction that that decision was for them the will of Christ. Throughout the centuries Christians have suffered and died for his sake and in this act of supreme devotion have found unspeakable joy in the thought that in their own suffering they partook of the suffering and the resurrection of their Lord. Humble and unlearned as well as sophisticated Christians have found a working guide for their practical conduct by asking the question, What would Jesus do if he were facing the decision I am about to make in my situation?

All these functions the church as a vital religious fellowship can perform, as the school, or, for that matter, any other institution, cannot. Relieved of the responsibility of attempting a program of religious instruction which it is ill equipped to carry out and which properly belongs to public education, the church can devote itself with intelligence and effectiveness to a program of religious nurture which by its essential nature it is equipped to carry on as no other institution can.

III

The concepts of the nature and ends of education, on the one hand, and of the functional relation of religion to experience, on the other, as set forth in chapter iii, require that ways be found for bringing into some form of effective co-operation all the agencies in the community that in one way or another affect the growth of persons. The purview of this discussion is for the most part limited to the relation of the church and the school in education. It is not our intention here to enter into a discussion of the relation of other agencies in the community to the major problem of religion in education.

The family, however, sustains such an intimate relation to both church and school, and its place in the religious nurture of the young is so fundamental, that it must receive brief consideration even though it lies beyond the limits of our present purpose. From the standpoint both of education and of religious nurture the family carries a major responsibility which cannot be delegated to any other institution. The family is the cell from which society grows. Through it not only is the biological continuity of the race achieved, but the cultural inheritance is passed on from the mature to the immature. For this reason the family is the oldest and most fundamental educational institution. The Catholics have good historical and social grounds for placing the family first in the hierarchy of educational agencies, especially for religious nurture.

The grounds for the importance of the family as a medium for religious nurture inhere in the nature of the family as a social institution. It is the view of many psychologists that the earliest years—perhaps the first three—are the most influential in shaping the emotional attitudes and behavior patterns that will persist throughout adult life. It is in the family that these early attitudes are formed. Here the child not only learns the "mother-tongue" but takes over the attitudes and habits of his parents and older brothers and sisters. Thus the family mediates the going culture into which he is born as it finds expression in the ways of thinking and acting of the members of this most intimate of all social groups.

Much of the effectiveness of the family as an agency of religious nurture lies in the fact that it is an intimate face-to-face group. In it the value of persons ideally transcends all other values. The relationships involved are deeply personal, concrete, intimate, and obvious. In the normal family the uniting bonds are mutual affection, understanding, and sympathy. In a well-ordered family the child has that sense of security and of belonging that is so essential to a happy and well-integrated personality, and he has a sense of a world that is ordered and governed by love. On the contrary, as is so often tragically the case, the broken family, or the family in which there is emotional conflict between parents, has devastating effects upon the mental and physical health of the child.

These influences operate not so much through formal training as through the child's unconscious participation in the family as a genuinely religious community. The religious influence of the family is operative to the degree that religious attitudes and values are genuine and sincere realities in the shared experience of the home. In the pioneer family these relationships had the immense advantage that they were mediated through common activities shared by parents and children, such as growing crops, baking bread, caring for animals, and providing for the manifold needs of the home.

As American life has developed, however, the family has undergone many changes that have tended to disrupt its close unity and to lessen its resources as an agency for religious nurture. The crowding of population in cities has thrown families into close contact and has weakened the once close-knit bonds of the home. The needs of the modern family are provided by services outside the home. The members of the family are drawn apart by vocation and recreation—a fragmentation greatly accentuated by the automobile. These conditions create new and difficult problems for the modern family. In addition to these structural changes the onetime specific religious activities of the home —such as the family altar, religious conversation, and elementary religious instruction—have for the most part disappeared. With the growing freedom of children and young people, parental discipline has declined. Parents themselves are confused. Few enlightened parents wish for the return of autocratic authority, but they have not yet arrived at the organization of the family on a democratic basis and the realization of new and better forms of domestic life under modern conditions.

The family is greatly in need of the intelligent and wholehearted co-operation of church and school in reinstating the home as the primary educational institution both for citizenship and for religious nurture. At the same time both church and school are in need of an equally intelligent and wholehearted co-operation on the part of parents. The cause of family, church, and school in guiding the experience of growing persons into competence in dealing with the living issues of contemporary life is one cause. Above all, parents, teachers, and churchmen need to sit down before the needs of their children and young people and to pool their resources in meeting these needs. This none of them can do working alone, nor all of them working separately.

In a similar way it would be possible to show the contribution which each of the social agencies has to make to the total education of childhood and youth and to their religious nurture. Even a cursory glance indicates their great opportunities and responsibilities. Some of these agencies have very direct contributions to make, as in the case of the child-guidance clinic, the juvenile court, social case work, relief agencies, leisure-time organizations, and the library. Perhaps it is not too much to envision the time when all these service agencies will discover a basis for the integration of their programs in the needs of persons and of the community which now in isolated ways they serve.

After this all-too-brief survey of the contributions which the school and the church, together with the family and other social agencies, have to make to the religious instruction and nurture of the young, we may conclude by restating the thesis of this study. It is that education in all its forms, including that having to do with religious nurture, is an affair of the community and not of any single institution. The responsibility for inducting the young into their cultural heritage, including their religious heritage, and for cultivating religious attitudes and motives is first and last a social responsibility. There is imperative need, therefore, that the base of education in religion, like that of all other forms of education, shall be drawn in the total life of the community. Around this new center of education it becomes the responsibility of the whole community to sit down before the needs of its children and young people, including their religious needs, and ask what it is that each agency has to contribute to a comprehensive and co-ordinated program of education for the whole self and for the whole community.

The community, in seeking to educate its young in the values which it most cherishes, will educate itself. For, when a community sets out to interpret its values to its young and to make these values effective in their lives, it will need to become aware of its operative values, to appraise them, to rectify them, and to create a scale of values that it can justify to itself. No community can communicate to its young people values that are not vital and compelling to itself. For, when all allowance has been made for technical educational procedures, the most vital education of children and young people comes about through their participation in the total life of the community.

A SELECTED BIBLIOGRAPHY

BOOKS

ADAMS, JAMES TRUSLOW. *The Living Jefferson.* New York: Charles Scribner's Sons, 1936.

AMES, EDWARD SCRIBNER. *Religion.* New York: Henry Holt & Co., 1929.

ARROWOOD, CHARLES FLINN (ed.). *Thomas Jefferson and Education in a Republic.* New York: McGraw-Hill Book Co., Inc., 1930.

BEARD, CHARLES A. *The Unique Function of Education in a Democracy.* Washington, D.C.: Educational Policies Commission, National Education Association, 1937.

BOWER, WILLIAM CLAYTON. *Character through Creative Experience.* Chicago: University of Chicago Press, 1930.

———. *Christ and Christian Education.* New York: Abingdon-Cokesbury Press, 1943.

——— (ed.). *The Church at Work in the Modern World.* Chicago: University of Chicago Press, 1935.

———. *Religion and the Good Life.* New York: Abingdon Press, 1933.

BROWN, WILLIAM ADAMS. *Church and State in Contemporary America.* New York: Charles Scribner's Sons, 1936.

BROWN, S. W. *The Secularization of American Education.* New York: Bureau of Publications, Teachers College, Columbia University, 1912.

CHAPMAN, J. C., and COUNTS, G. S. *Principles of Education.* Boston: Houghton Mifflin Co., 1924.

Character Education. Washington, D.C.: Department of Superintendence, 1932.

Christian Education Today. Chicago: International Council of Religious Education, 1940.

COE, GEORGE A. *Educating for Citizenship.* New York: Charles Scribner's Sons, 1932.

———. *Law and Freedom in the School.* Chicago: University of Chicago Press, 1924.

———. *The Psychology of Religion.* Chicago: University of Chicago Press, 1916.

———. *What Is Religion Doing to Our Consciences?* New York: Charles Scribner's Sons, 1943.

CUBBERLEY, ELLWOOD P. *Public Education in the United States.* Boston: Houghton Mifflin Co., 1919.

DAVIS, M. D. *Weekday Classes in Religious Education on Released Time for Public School Pupils.* Washington, D.C.: U.S. Office of Education, 1941.

ROY J. DEFERRARI (ed.). *Essays on Catholic Education in the United States.* Washington, D.C.: Catholic University of America Press, 1942.

————. *Vital Problems of Catholic Education in the United States.* Washington, D.C.: Catholic University of America Press, 1939.

DEWEY, JOHN. *A Common Faith.* New Haven, Conn.: Yale University Press, 1934.

————. *The Living Thoughts of Thomas Jefferson.* New York: Longman's Green & Co., 1940.

————. *Moral Principles in Education.* Boston: Houghton Mifflin Co., 1909.

The Essential Place of Religion in Education. Ann Arbor: National Education Association, 1916.

EVERETT, SAMUEL (ed.). *The Community School.* New York: D. Appleton–Century Co., 1938.

HARTMAN, G. W. *Educational Psychology.* New York: American Book Co., 1941.

HARTSHORNE, HUGH. *Character in Human Relations.* New York: Charles Scribner's Sons, 1932.

HENDERSON, J. C. *Thomas Jefferson's Views on Education.* New York: G. P. Putnam's Sons, 1890.

HINSDALE, B. A. *Horace Mann and the Common School Revival in the United States.* New York: Charles Scribner's Sons, 1898.

HOPKINS, L. THOMAS, *et al. Integration: Its Meaning and Application.* New York: D. Appleton–Century Co., 1937.

JACKSON, J. C., and MALMBERG, C. F. *Religious Education and the State.* New York: Doubleday, Doran & Co., 1928.

JOURNET, CHARLES. *La Juridiction de l'église sur la cité.* Paris: Desclée de Broewer & Cie, 1931.

KEESECKER, W. W. *Legal Status of Bible Reading and Religious Instruction in Public Schools.* Washington, D.C.: U.S. Government Printing Office, 1930.

LOTZ, P. H., and CRAWFORD, L. W. *Studies in Religious Education.* Nashville: Cokesbury Press, 1931.

MANN, HORACE. *The Common School Controversy.* Boston: J. N. Bradley & Co., 1844.

MARITAIN, J. *Religion et culture.* Paris: Desclée de Broewer & Cie, 1930.

MOEHLMAN, CONRAD H. *The American Constitutions and Religion.* Berne, Ind.: Privately published, 1938.

PLANT, JAMES S. *Personality and the Cultural Pattern.* New York: Commonwealth Fund, 1937.

REAVIS, WILLIAM C. (ed.). *The School and the Urban Community.* Chicago: University of Chicago Press, 1943.

RUGG, HAROLD. *American Life and the School Curriculum.* New York: Ginn & Co., 1936.

Rugg, Harold (ed.). *Democracy and the Curriculum*. New York: D. Appleton–Century Co., 1939.

Smith, Henry L. *Character Development through Moral and Religious Education in the Public Schools of the United States*. Bloomington: University of Indiana Press, 1937.

Smith, Payson; Winship, A. E.; and Harris, W. T. *Thomas Mann and Our Schools*. New York: American Book Co., 1937.

Smith, S. M. *The Relation of the State to Religious Education*. Syracuse, N.Y.: Syracuse University Press, 1926.

Ulrich, Robert. *Foundations of Education in a Democracy*. New York: American Book Co., 1940.

Van Dusen, Henry P., *et al. Church and State in the Modern World*. New York: Harper & Bros., 1937.

Wiltse, C. M. *Thomas Jefferson: A Study in the Philosophy of the State*. Ithaca, N.Y., 1932.

Zachry, Caroline B. *Personality Adjustments of School Children*. New York: Charles Scribner's Sons, 1929.

PERIODICALS

Beard, Charles A. "Democracy and Education in the United States," *Social Research*, September, 1937.

Beman, L. T. "Religious Teaching in Public Schools," *The Reference Shelf*, Vol. V, No. 2 (June, 1927).

Bower, W. C. "Religious Education and the Psychology of Religion," *Religious Education*, January, 1928.

———. "The Nature and Function of Religion," *ibid.*, April, 1936.

Butler, Nicholas M. "Place of Religious Instruction in Our Educational System," *Vital Speeches*, January 1, 1941.

Coe, G. A. "Shall the State Teach Religion?" *School and Society*, February 3, 1940.

Coe, G. A., and Johnson, F. E. "Discussion of Religion in Public Education," *International Journal of Religious Education*, September, 1941; October, 1941; November, 1941; December, 1941.

Fox, George G. "Old Issue in a New Guise: Merger of Church and State," *Christian Century*, August 20, 1941.

Hart, J. K. "Religion in the Schools? Yes!" *School and Society*, March 15, 1925.

Johnson, F. Ernest. "Religion and the Philosophy of Education," *Vital Speeches*, November 1, 1940.

Kepner, C. W. "School Challenges the Church," *School and Society*, September 21, 1940.

McCasland, S. V. "Our Secularized Education," *Christian Century*, December 17, 1941.

McKibben, Frank M. "Religious Backing in Public Education," *International Journal of Religious Education*, November 13, 1939.

Mann, Louis. "Limitations of Public Education: The Jewish View," *Religious Education*, June, 1927.

Morrison, Charles Clayton. "The Inner Citadel of Democracy," *Christian Century*, May 7 and 14, 1942.

Newcomb, R. S. "Introducing Moral and Religious Instruction in the Public School," *Elementary School Journal*, June, 1926.

Robinson, E. A. "Stanford Conference on Religion in Higher Education," *School and Society*, June 6, 1942.

Shattuck, G. E. "Religious Education in the Schools," *School and Society*, March 22, 1941.

Tuttle, C. H. "Public Schools and Religious Education," *Vital Speeches*, February 15, 1940.

Weigle, Luther A. "Public Education and Religion," *Religious Education*, April–June, 1940.

INDEX

Ames, Edward S., 31

American life: concept of democracy in, 15–16; cultural changes in, 17–18; dynamic, 11; foundations of, laid in religious faith, 23; frontier of, 13–14; growth of national community, 13–14; growth of technology in, 12–13; industrialization of, 12–13; involvement of, in international relations, 16, 17, 19, 20; population changes in, 12; secularization of, 2, 17, 28; territorial expansion of, 11–12; great changes in, 4–6

Beneš, Eduard, 19

Bible, 24, 29, 61

Brown, S. W., 29

Brown, William Adams, 69

Butler, Nicholas M., 43

Calhoun, R. L., 55

Catholic education, 35–36

Catholics, 8, 28, 34, 35–36, 51

Celebrations, 67–68

Ceremonials, 47, 67–68

Chave, Ernest J., 66

Christianity, 48–49

Church: corporateness of, 79–80, 86; disestablishment of, in New England and Virginia, 53; establishment of, 5–6; explicates religious values, 81–82; a fellowship, 83, 85, 88; function of, in education, 78–95; gives sense of at-homeness in universe, 83–85; present educational program of, unsatisfactory, 58–59; provides causes, 88–91; provides stimulating environment, 87–88; sets life in universal context, 82–83

Church and state, 5, 6, 28, 53–54, 55–56, 59, 60; both grounded in the community, 54; functionally related, 53–54; institutionally separate, 53–54; separation of, 6, 28, 59, 60

Coe, George A., 31

Colonial education: religious, 23–25; diversity of, 24–25

Commitment, 90

Community: center of education, 46; church and state grounded in, 54–56; education of, 94–95; as ultimate social reality, 54

Community agencies, 46

Concern regarding relation of religion to education, 1, 2, 41

Co-operation: of community agencies, 91, 94; of Protestants, 7–9; of Protestants, Catholics, and Jews, 8

Cubberley, E. P., 29

Culture: atomism of, 68–70, 83; integration of, 17; religion a phase of, 8, 30–32, 47–48, 49, 59; unbalanced American, 17–18

Deferrari, Roy G., 36

De Lima, Agnes, 42

Democracy: concept of, 5, 6, 15, 16; education for, 34, 75; re-examination of, 19, and religion, 34–35

Department of Superintendence, 2

Dewey, John, 44, 52

Disestablishment: in New England, 53; in Virginia, 53

Durkheim, Émile, 31

Education: centered in the community, 46; as discipline, 42–43; European backgrounds of, 5; a function of democracy, 3; as guided experience, 44–46; nature and ends of, 5, 41–46; and the new world order, 19–21; as recapitulation, 43–44; situation of, in America, 22–41; a social function, 30; as transmission of knowledge, 43

Educational situation in America: diversity of, 24–25; earliest educa-

[101]

tion in America, 23–25; reaction of churches to exclusion of religion, 35–39; reaction of schools to exclusion of religion, 39–40; results of exclusion of religion, 30–35; secularization of education, 25–28

European backgrounds: of American life, 5, 23; of education, 5, 23–24, 36

Exclusion of religion from public schools: reaction of churches to, 35–39; reaction of schools to, 39–40; result of sectarianism, 28–29, 53; results of, 30–35

Experimentation needed, 75

Family, the, 91–94

Federal Council of the Churches of Christ in America, 7, 9

Froebel, F. W. A., 44

Frontier: factor in American life, 13–14; factor in secularization of education, 26–27

Fundamental assumptions: a functional concept of education, 41–46; a functional concept of relation of church and state, 53–56; a functional concept of religion, 47–53

Giddings, Franklin H., 30

Gideonse, H. D., 69

God, 50, 51, 56, 82, 86, 87, 88

Government, 54–55

Hall, G. Stanley, 43

Hamilton, Alexander, 6

Haskell, Edward F., 63

Herbart, J. F., 43

Higher education, 40

Hoover, Herbert, 17

Hutchins, Robert Maynard, 69

Huxley, Aldous, 19

Integration: factors of, in culture, 69–70; need of, in education, 68; religion as a factor of, 69–70

International Council of Religious Education, 8, 9

Isolationism, 16–17

Jefferson, Thomas, 6, 12, 23, 76

Jesus, 65, 89, 90, 91

Jews: education of, 38–39; religion of, 48, 50, 51

Jung, C. G., 33, 70

Lincoln, Abraham, 75

Locke, John, 42

Lutherans, 35

Macmurray, John, 66

Mann, Horace, 23, 28, 76

Mathews, Shailer, 7, 8, 51

Morrison, Charles Clayton, 69

Neo-orthodoxy, 51, 82

New world order, 19, 21

Niebuhr, Richard, 48

Ogburn, William F., 17

Parochial schools, 24, 35–36, 37

Personal counseling, 70–71

Pestalozzi, J. H., 44

Practical difficulties: method, 72; minority groups, 71; not insuperable, 71–72; pressure groups, 71; and sectarian attitudes of teachers, 71

Presbyterian experiment in parochial schools, 36

President of the United States, 2

Pressure groups, 71

Problem of religion and education: arises out of needs of young people and nation, 4; early solution of, not satisfactory, 28–29; an old problem in a new setting, 1–21; outgrowth of national history, 4; requires re-examination, 5, 22–23, 30, 57; underlying concepts of, 5, 41–56

Protestant education, 36–38

Protestants, 7, 8, 34

Public school: authentic interpreter of American culture, 60; authorities, 1, 2, 41; experiencing religious values in school situations, 65–67; not godless, 76; personal counseling in, 70–71; religion as a field of knowledge in, 63–65; religion may be taught as a part of curriculum of, 60–63; use of ceremonials and celebrations in, 67–68

Reaction: of churches to exclusion of religion, 35–39; of schools to exclusion of religion, 39–40

Religion: changes in, 6–11; co-operation in, 7–9; and democracy, 34–35; exclusion of, from public schools, 6, 28, 30, 53; a factor in cultural integration, 68–70; a form of social behavior, 73; function of, to be distinguished from its instruments, 51–52; a functional concept of, 47–53; a historical process, 48–49; an integral part of school program, 1, 2, 57–77; nature and function of, 5, 47–53; a phase of culture, 8, 30–32, 47–48, 49, 59; scientific study of, 9, 10, 47; secularization of, 52; a valuational experience, 10, 49–50; in the White House Conference, 2, 3

Religion and education: a changing problem, 22, 23; contribution of the church to, 78–91; contribution of the school to, 57–77; a new problem, 3, 4, 23; relation of, needs re-examination, 21; a unique problem in America, 22

Revolution, American, 5, 22

Sectarianism: characteristic of American religion, 47; disruption of schools by, 6; factor in secularization of education, 28–29; follows social stratification, 48; grounds of disappearing, 6–9; identifies theology, ritual, and ecclesiasticism with religion, 52; incapacitates church for education, 78–79; may become secular, 52; not admissible in schools, 59; responsible for exclusion of religion from schools, 53; rights of sectarian bodies, 59, 80; stereotypes of, 9, 10, 17

Secular, the: and religion, 52; religious significance of, 9

Secularization of American education: factors of, 26–28; influence of the expanding demands of culture upon, 26–27; influence of the frontier upon, 26–27; influence of mixed population upon, 27–28; sectarianism a cause of, 28

Sheldon, William H., 31

Sherrill, Lewis J., 36

Smith, Alfred E., 54

"Social Creed of the Churches," 9

Social reconstruction, 9

Sunday school, 36–37

Symbols, 88

Teachers: attitude of, 71; professional training of, 1, 72; religious character of, 76–77

Theology: development of, 51; differences in, 6–8; function of, 81–82; reflection upon religious experience, 31; stereotypes of, 9, 71

Thomas, W. I., 85

Totalitarian states, 19, 34, 35

Unified science, the religious implications of, 61–63

Union movements, 7

Vacation church schools, 36, 37

Values: center of religious experience, 9–10; central in modern religious education, 8–9; need of, in education, 20, 21; operative, 95, potential, 85; in school relations, 65–67;

Van Dusen, H. P., 55

Weekday church school, 36, 37–38, 39

Wells, H. G., 18

White House Conference, 2, 3, 8

Wilson, Woodrow, 43

World Council of Churches, 7

World War, 19, 20

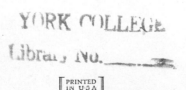

THE school, better than the home, better than any special agency, better than even the denominational church, can teach the content of religion and give children the experience of religious values involved in everyday relationships. This is the heart of Mr. Bower's argument for the need of teaching religion in the public schools.

The first American schools included religious instruction as a natural and vital part of their programs. Later, however, sectarianism caused the exclusion of religion from the public schools. This was the beginning of the problem of religion in education. Today it has become one of the most pressing problems in American life.

Shall we continue to neglect the religious needs of children and young people? In the light of a century and a half of experience, the fundamental concepts underlying the problem are re-examined—the relation of church and state, the nature and ends of education as a social process, and the functional relation of religion to personal and social experience. On the basis of this examination, Mr. Bower makes his decision and proposes a constructive solution.

The roots of modern democracy are deeply imbedded in religion, with its emphasis upon the worth of persons and the